Blessed Is the Man

A Man's Journey through the Psalms

Psalms of Divine Wisdom

Praise the LORD!
Blessed is the man
who fears the LORD,
who greatly delights
in His commandments!

Psalm 112:1

Copyright © 2009 Concordia Publishing House

3558 S. Jefferson Ave., St. Louis, MO 63118-3968

1-800-325-3040 • www.cph.org

All rights reserved. No part of this publication may be reproduced, stored in a retrieval system, or transmitted,
in any form or by any means, electronic, mechanical, photocopying, recording, or otherwise,
without the prior written permission of Concordia Publishing House.

By Joel D. Biermann, Tim Radkey, Matt Victor, John Crowe, Frank Fischer, Bob Morris, Steve Sandfort, and Gary Dunker

Edited by Robert C. Baker

Unless otherwise indicated, Scripture quotations are from The Holy Bible, English Standard Version®. Copyright © 2001
by Crossway Bibles, a publishing ministry of Good News Publishers, Wheaton, Illinois. Used by permission. All rights reserved.

Scripture quotations marked NASB are taken from the New American Standard Bible®. NIV®. Copyright © 1960, 1962, 1963, 1968,
1971, 1972, 1973, 1975, 1977, 1995 by The Lockman Foundation. Used by permission. (www.Lockman.org)

Quotations from *Reading the Psalms with Luther*, copyright © 2007 Concordia Publishing House. All rights reserved.

The definition of *Sacrament* on page 208 is adapted from *Luther's Small Catechism with Explanation*,
copyright © 1986, 1991 Concordia Publishing House, pp. 202–203.

This publication may be available in braille, in large print, or on cassette tape for the visually impaired.
Please allow 8 to 12 weeks for delivery. Write to Lutheran Blind Mission, 7550 Watson Rd., St. Louis, MO 63119-4409;
call toll free 1-888-215-2455; or visit the Web site: www.blindmission.org.

1 2 3 4 5 6 7 8 9 10   18 17 16 15 14 13 12 11 10 09

Contents

Meet Our Authors

Joel D. Biermann

Joel resides in St. Louis, Missouri, with his bride of 24 years, Jeannalee. Their two daughters, Jasmine and Justine, are Lutheran school teachers, and their son Jess is enjoying his formative high school years. Joel's vocation finds him at Concordia Seminary, St. Louis, teaching Systematic Theology. Leading the list of favorite pastimes is any active outdoor pursuit with Jeannalee, who excels at providing what is best for Joel and their family.

Tim Radkey

Tim, his wife Lea Ann, and their five-year-old daughter, Claire, reside in Lubbock, Texas, where Tim serves as senior pastor of Hope Lutheran Church. Tim has written and appeared in several DVD-based Bible studies produced by LHM's Men's Network. On weekends, Tim and his family enjoy spending time in the mountains of New Mexico. Tim also runs marathons, rides bicycles, and rides around town on his new Harley Davidson.

Matt Victor

Matt has been married to his wife, Carol, for 25 years, and they are blessed with three wonderful kids. Matt was born and raised in the Jewish tradition and was brought to faith in Christ in 1989, at age 30. Matt has worked in the information technology industry for the past twenty-five years having a variety of responsibilities. Matt says, "As with most folks, we have had our ups and downs over the years, but the Lord has always carried us through."

John Crowe

John and his wife, Sandra, are the parents of five children. He serves as parish administrator at St. John Lutheran Church and School in Wheaton, Illinois. In his spare time John teaches and plays tennis, and enjoys singing in his church's choir and in small ensembles. Holding degrees from Valparaiso University and the University of Phoenix, John is working on lay ministry certification through Concordia University, Mequon, Wisconsin.

Frank Fischer

Frank married his high school prom date, who has been his best friend for 31 years. Frank and his wife have a daughter, 28, and a son, 26, Frank is a 30-plus-year veteran of the logistics and supply chain field and now operates his own third party logistics enterprise. Frank enjoys fishing, woodworking, singing in the choir, and voluteering to serve our Lord in a variety of capacities at St. John Lutheran Church in Ellisville, Missouri.

Bob Morris

Bob has been married for 40 years, has three children and two grandchildren. He retired as a colonel from the U.S. Air Force after 26 years of service. Bob is now a private pilot. Among many public service activities, Bob serves as president of The Gideons International, West Madison County, Illinois; is a tour guide for the U.S. Army Corps of Engineers Lock and Dam 26, Mississippi River; and is a volunteer at National Great Rivers Museum, near Alton, Illinois.

Steve Sandfort

Steve and his wife, Becky, and their three children live in Fort Wayne, Indiana. Following 11 years in church work and 8 years as a professional actor and recording artist, Steven has settled into the life of a seminary student at Concordia Theological Seminary. Steve speaks and performs at LCMS events, and works on film and television when his schedule permits. He and Becky homeschool their children. You can visit Steve at stevesandfort.com.

Gary Dunker

Gary and his wife, Carol, live in Lincoln, Nebraska, where they worship at Messiah Lutheran Church. Gary works in sales for KLCV Radio, a member of the Christian Bott Radio Network. Gary enjoys attending Nebraska football and baseball games, writing adult Bible studies and dramas, as well as spending time with his four grand-children Evan, Easton, Brynley, and Dathin.

How to Use This Book

This isn't your father's devotional.

Then again, while your father may not have read the stories found in *Blessed Is the Man*, he may have heard stories similar to them. Stories told by his father or brother or friend, real stories from real men who experienced real life relying on God's real—and amazing—grace. Stories like the ones you've heard other believers tell you, or stories you've told yourself.

Blessed Is the Man provides you and your Bible study group with six weeks of faith narratives written by men who have prayerfully considered biblical psalms. At the beginning of each week, you will read an assigned psalm. Five days during that week you'll read a verse or two of that psalm, followed by the author's story. Next, you may pray a suggested prayer or choose another as you see fit. Finally, you'll answer a few brief Bible study questions, which will help you consider other ways the psalm may apply to you. To get the most out of *Blessed Is the Man*, prayerfully review the psalm from time to time throughout the week. Through God's Word, the Holy Spirit will confront and challenge, but He will also comfort and console. At the end of each week, join your brothers in Christ in a group Bible study. Weekly small-group questions are reproducible. So, if you want to hold your group Bible study before hammering the first nail at a Habitat for Humanity project, at halftime during a televised game, or before you throw the brats on the grill, do so! You may make as many copies of these pages as you need for the guys in your group.

We are grateful that you are taking a man's journey through the Psalms in *Blessed Is the Man*. Along the way, you may be reminded of stories of faith told by your grandfather, father, brother, or friend. The adventure into God's Word may even inspire you to tell a few on your own.

—The Editor

Suggestions for Small-Group Participants

1. Before you begin, spend some time in prayer, asking God to strengthen your faith through a study of His Word. The Scriptures were written so that we might believe in Jesus Christ and have life in His name (John 20:31).

2. Take some time before the meeting to look over the session, review the psalm, and answer the questions.

3. As a courtesy to others, arrive on time.

4. Be an active participant. The leader will guide the group's discussion, not give a lecture.

5. Avoid dominating the conversation by answering every question or by giving unnecessarily long answers. On the other hand, avoid the temptation to not share at all.

6. Treat anything shared in your group as confidential until you have asked for and received permission to share it outside of the group. Treat information about others outside of your group as confidential until you have asked for and received permission to share it with group members.

7. Some participants may be new to Bible study or new to the Christian faith. Help them feel welcome and comfortable.

8. Affirm other participants when you can. If someone offers what you perceive to be a "wrong" answer, ask the Holy Spirit to guide him to seek the correct answer from God's Word.

9. Keep in mind that the questions are discussion starters. Don't be afraid to ask additional questions that relate to the topic. Don't get the group off track.

10. If you are comfortable doing so, volunteer now and then to pray at the beginning or end of the session.

Guide to Men's Ministry

There's a mother watching her boys play in the backyard. The boys are wrestling around in the mud, fighting to see who will be at the top of the pecking order, as brothers often do. There's another mother in the same backyard who has a little girl, or you might even say a *princess*. She comments, "Don't you think those boys are going to hurt one another? How are you going to get the stains out of their clothes?" To this, the mother of the boys replies, "Boys will be boys." In this short story, it is clear that one mother understands boys and the other has no clue how boys become men.

The sad news is this: the Church in many ways has adopted the voice of the princess's mother who never raised boys. It seems men are expected to live, act, and behave in ways that makes sure any remnant of their childhood has been extinguished. Men are tamed to fit the mold of what a good little boy should look like— free of danger, free of risk, and free of anything fun.

Giving men permission to be men once again is absolutely critical to the Church and to a successful men's ministry. There is enough boy left in every man that beckons to compete, have fun, risk, and live out the adventurous spirit only God can give. Yes, it is possible for all of this to happen in the Church while men still live within the will and call of God upon their lives.

7 Tips for Men's Ministry

GET "REAL" LEADERS

Men desperately need leaders who are authentic, genuine, and nonjudgmental. You must choose a leader whom other men would want to hang out with and can relate to on multiple levels. This is a guy who other guys love to hang out with because he seems so down to earth, has fun living life, and would be a leader in any environment he found himself in.

THERA-PUKE-IC

Guys need to be in an environment that is natural, not clinical. Guys will share their struggles, challenges, and victories as long as it's not the purpose of the meeting or even the hidden agenda for their time together. When they catch wind that this is about to turn into group therapy, most guys will immediately button their lips, turn off their brain, and look for the nearest exit. When the environment is right, guys will talk. Don't force it. Please, don't force it.

LESS IS MORE

Women are always amazed at how simple men can be at times. Most men like simplicity and are drawn to it. Whether you're planning a men's social, Bible study, retreat, or small group, it is always better to err on the side of keeping it simple. Simple doesn't mean plain or boring; it means doing a few things really, really well. When you sit down to plan activities, try structuring them around broader themes such as having fun, learning a little, and providing a good challenge or risk for men to participate in.

TALKING IS OPTIONAL

Generally when men come together for activities, Bible studies, small groups, and/or retreats, there is going to be a time for prayer, reading, and answering some questions. There are many men who don't like to read out loud, pray out loud, or be put on the spot to answer questions out loud. Be sure to check with guys ahead of time about praying or reading. There will always be a few men who are comfortable answering questions, and these men usually pave the way for more timid guys to speak up.

KEEP THE SPIRIT OF COMPETITION ALIVE

Not all men played sports, but most men have competed as boys in some area or another. Men, by and large, enjoy competition and friendly wagers. Some men like playing golf against one another, while others enjoy seeing who smokes the best brisket. Either way you slice it, men always enjoy themselves when they can compete in a nonthreatening way, in a way that will never leave them feeling foolish in front of each other.

MEETINGS SHOULD NEVER BE MEETINGS

From time to time, there will be a need to plan various activities for men. The worst thing you can do is form a committee or a board. There will always be natural leaders who will need to do some planning for men's ministry, but have the meeting at a place men enjoy, like an athletic event, a pub, or even on a golf course while playing a round. No one, especially men, needs to add more "official" meetings to his schedule. Make it informal and fun while you orchestrate real business.

A MINISTRY NEEDS MORE THAN ONE DOOR

How accessible is your ministry? The fastest growing churches always have multiple entry points for folks to get involved and be connected to their church. Men's ministry is no different. While there is a tremendous brotherhood among men, there are also a wide range of things that men like and don't like. Some men like camping and the great outdoors. Other men would prefer manual labor around the church. Some might even like more intellectually oriented activities. No matter what, you need to ensure that your men's ministry has many different attractions that respect different interests, gifts, abilities, and skills. There are venues for all men to come together, and there are activities that will only attract certain men. Keep all these nuances in mind.

3 Steps to Launch a
Men's Ministry in *Your* Church

LOCATION, LOCATION, LOCATION

Pick a place that will work for launching your first men's ministry event. A tailgate setting would be an absolutely prime site. Other options are at a lake, the rustic outdoors, or even a barn of sorts. Whatever you choose as your site, it should be a place where guys can get excited and loud and not feel closed in.

MEN EAT MEAT AND LOTS OF IT

Once you've got the location nailed down, it's time to think about the meat you are going to serve. Depending on what area of the country you live in, your choices and preferences will vary. Some examples are having a wild-game type spread of food. This usually takes place in areas where men enjoy hunting. If you have chosen a tailgate at some sporting event, cook up a bunch of bratwurst, brisket, and/or ribs. Warning: it's tough to cook a great steak when you're doing it in large numbers. Men are picky with their steaks, so be careful if this is your choice. Don't forget to bring beverages that your men would enjoy as well. (Okay, you can throw on some veggie burgers too.)

IT'S TIME TO LAUNCH—THE DAY IS HERE

Okay, you've chosen a great site. You've got the volunteers you need to cook the meat at the site. Now it's time to plan how you are going to effectively brainstorm what your men's ministry might look like. This is not a time to be critical of ideas. This is a time to really listen to what men are saying.

What kinds of activities do they want to be involved with?

What kinds of adventures are they looking for?

What contribution do they want their men's ministry to make to the kingdom of God externally and their church internally?

Make this fun. For example, to get things started you could have some balloons attached to a big piece of plywood and have various ideas written on paper inside of the balloons. Have one of the men use the BB gun you provided to shoot one of the balloons and see what idea is inside and talk about it. This exercise can be a lot of fun, but please be safe with it. Once you have some good ideas about the direction the men would like to go, pick another location to flush out more of the details and planning. Ask for any volunteers who want to help with this next phase. Once this next phase is finished, you should be able to get to work—but don't forget to keep on listening to the men in your church.

Joel D. Biermann

Introduction

"Read the Psalms."

Over the years, I have exhorted countless friends and acquaintances with those three words. I continue to give the same advice to people who find themselves in a tight place or facing some hard dilemma or sorrow. I suppose that one could hear the words as little more than a trite spiritual cliché pressed into service when there is nothing else insightful or helpful to say—along the same lines as "I'll pray for you." After all, directing a man in the midst of a crisis or difficult situation to read (anything!) demonstrates precious little imagination, compassion, or grasp of reality. Nevertheless, I did it and I still do it, not because I can think of nothing better to say or suggest or because I am overly optimistic about the capacity of men to choose to read but because actually reading the Psalms is such a meaningful and fruitful thing to do, especially during tough times. I give the counsel not with a twinge of guilt or regret for not having shown more compassion but with a note of hope and anticipation—as if I have just divulged a secret with the power to transform a man's life. And that, of course, is precisely the truth of the matter.

The collected Psalms of Israel constituted a large part of the worship life of God's Old Testament people. We have here the songs sung by worshipers in the temple and synagogue, songs sung by travelers wending their way up to Jerusalem to celebrate another festival, songs sung by ordinary people in their daily routines—an earworm stuck in their brain, rehearsing all day long the wonder of God's grace, the majesty of His creation, and the wisdom of His Law. The Psalms are starkly and rudely honest. When David is tired or worried or frustrated or worn out by life, God knows it . . . and so do we. That's the particular wonder of the Psalms and the power they have for us who read them today.

The Psalms teach us that there really is nothing new under the sun and that what we think must be a one-in-a-million struggle or heartache is actually the common plight of men in every time—and we marvel to discover that someone has already worked that moment of hard reality into a poignant, sometimes eloquent, and always truthful cry of faith. When you read the Psalms, that cry of faith becomes your cry of faith. Such is the latent power of the Psalms. They are the words of the Holy Spirit, inspired indeed, but they are also the words of real men, human and frail. The Psalms allow us to pray and praise along with these saints and to complain and question along with these sinners. They are both, of course, and so are we.

The Psalms, like life, are not all alike. Some are exuberant outbursts of praise, others are sad laments, still others focus on God's messianic promise, and yet another group takes up the realities of life in this world from the perspective of the Creator of this world. This book will center its attention on that final category, psalms that have been labeled wisdom psalms. It is a fitting name. In these psalms, we are led to consider God's plans for His people—specifically for His men. Yes, there is practical advice, but more than that, there is a perspective that can shape the way that all of life is seen.

So, you are poised to become a reader of the Psalms, not only a reader though, but also a studier, a slow digester of the Psalms. An entire six weeks devoted to six wisdom psalms is a leisurely pace, no doubt. But that's the beauty of the study. No need to hurry, no quotas to reach, no minimum of chapters to consume. Each day you consider a mere handful of verses, usually only one or two, and learn the truth of that word of God. You contemplate and consider its applications to your own life. And these psalms do their work. Please understand, the study that follows does not offer itself as a work of precise and careful exegesis or biblical interpretation. There is no pretence in these pages. This is a devotional work, an exercise in meditation and reflection on words of a text as they do real work in the present.

The very premise of the Psalms, then, finds its accurate echo in the format of this study. The psalm designated for each week is broken into five parts, one each for the workdays of the week. Each section is the basis of a devotional reflection written by ordinary men—men like you. These are men who live regular lives with regular jobs and regular struggles. And it is out of this regular ordinariness of mundane daily life that they write their meditations about the meaning of the verses. These are the thoughts and the insights of men like you, men like David, who simply lived their lives and in the living encountered God's reality. The strength of the Psalms is their ability to appeal to every man. That is also the strength of the devotional pieces that make up this volume. As you read along, you will join a contemporary brother in the faith and live life with him for a time. You will ride on horseback with a trail boss, cringe over the guilt of stolen money, marvel at the crazy grace of a mulligan, scour a black Nebraska backyard for night crawlers, get smitten from above by a plummeting Christmas star, and face the thrill and terror of piloting a plane. As you travel for a while with each author, you will learn with him valuable lessons about God and life—an experience not unlike reading the Psalms.

Reading the Psalms and benefitting from the experiences and thoughts of others who read can give you insight into life and its often hard realities. Better than that, reading the Psalms can help to reorient your life and its priorities. The Psalms have a way of calling us back to what matters. They compel us to take seriously God's call on our lives. And so it is that the real goal is not reading the Psalms but being read by the Psalms. The difference is profound. Those who merely read are looking for nuggets of wisdom, an insight into a thorny dilemma, a bit of comfort for a sad situation. Those who only read are trying to get something they can take on their own terms, something that can be fit into their life and its comfortable routine. By contrast, those who go to the Psalms to be read by the Psalms recognize the claim of the Psalms—these texts are the vehicle of the Holy Spirit. They are God's. They are normative. They are the standard. They are the reality into which we must fit our lives, not vice versa. The Psalms—especially the wisdom psalms—spell out what God expects. They give us the pattern. They call us to impossible heights and demand absurd sacrifices. They take our comfortable lives and rattle them—no, batter them into a broken shambles—challenging our even-keel, unruffled existence and forcing us to see things with new eyes: God's eyes. Such is the disconcerting experience of being read by the Psalms. When the text reads the man, the man cannot stay the same. He must change or die resisting.

Martin Luther insisted—and taught all of us—that the center of Scripture is Christ. This is, as he also knew, intensely true of the Psalms—even the wisdom psalms. But it is not as if one must look beneath every verse of each psalm to find Christ somehow hidden in an obscure analogy or in some sort of gospel-trickery that manufactures Christological implications where none are present. No, our Lord is present in the text as He Himself speaks the text to us. Our Lord is present and the center as He alone is able to embody the descriptions of the righteous and blessed man who lives always and fully within the will of the Father. Our Lord is most certainly and mercifully present as He comes to us who have endured being read by the text—who have been undone in our self-deluded satisfaction and equanimity—and delivers to us the delicious grace of undeserved and unfathomable forgiveness. This is the way that Christ is present for us, and this is the way that Christ is truly the living and life-giving center of every wisdom psalm.

Blessed Is the Man is an apt title. For we who read the Psalms—and far more important, we who are read by the Psalms—are truly blessed when the Psalms reduce us to nothingness, only to assure us again of God's gracious favor made certain in the life, death, and resurrection of the One who alone is the blessed Man. We are His people, and as His people we share what is His—even His blessedness. The blessed man is a breathtaking standard. That is true. But the blessed man is also the promise of God. It is what He works in His people through the power of the Spirit. It is what He works in you who read and are read by the Psalms. So, press forward with anticipation. You are about to become a reader of the Psalms. Better yet, you are about to become one who is read by the Psalms. And so it will be true and be said of you: blessed is the man.

Week One

Psalm 112

[1] Praise the LORD!
Blessed is the man who fears the LORD,
who greatly delights in His commandments!

[2] His offspring will be mighty in the land;
the generation of the upright will be blessed.

[3] Wealth and riches are in his house,
and his righteousness endures forever.

[4] Light dawns in the darkness for the upright;
he is gracious, merciful, and righteous.

[5] It is well with the man who deals generously and lends;
who conducts his affairs with justice.

[6] For the righteous will never be moved;
he will be remembered forever.

[7] He is not afraid of bad news;
his heart is firm, trusting in the LORD.

[8] His heart is steady; he will not be afraid,
until he looks in triumph on his adversaries.

[9] He has distributed freely; he has given to the poor;
his righteousness endures forever;
his horn is exalted in honor.

[10] The wicked man sees it and is angry;
he gnashes his teeth and melts away;
the desire of the wicked will perish!

Matt Victor

Psalm 112:1-2

Praise the LORD! Blessed is the man who fears the LORD, who greatly delights in His commandments! His offspring will be mighty in the land; the generation of the upright will be blessed.

A Different Kind of Fear

On September 11, 2001, there was more than enough fear to go around. Only one block from the World Trade Center that day, I was afraid like never before in my life. I watched in horror as people jumped nearly a hundred stories to their deaths, flames lapping at their backs as they fell. I prayed, "Lord, I pray that they know You and Your saving grace." As the day's events unfolded before my eyes, I called on the Lord through prayer numerous times. September 11 impacted my family well into the future, but God would lead us through the emotional and financial challenges that lay ahead with His grace.

When you hear the word *fear*, what do you think of? Are you afraid of being alone in the dark? Do snakes make the hair stand up on the back of your neck? There is another kind of fear that is used many times in the Bible. Psalm 112:1 tells us "Blessed is the man who fears the LORD." This kind of fear is different than the fear we normally experience. It's not the kind of fear that I and many others experienced on 9/11. The fear that I am talking about is a God-given, deep respect for Him and His undeserved love toward us. Instead of running away from this fear, we should embrace it.

You and I live in a sin-soaked world. We sometimes struggle to stay afloat. Our minds can become cluttered with all of the things we need to do. Whether it is that special work project that always gets delayed or that unbudgeted bill that arrived this month, challenges confront us. And how do we react? Usually we try to maintain our self-image. We say to ourselves, "I can handle this. Let me put in a few more hours at work," or "I really had my heart set on that iPod. That bill is just going to have to wait."

Now don't get me wrong; sometimes we do have to take the proverbial "bull by the horns." But we also need to remember Who really is in charge. Too often, when things start whirling out of control, we focus on ourselves and lose sight of who can help us. We turn our focus away from Jesus and start putting our faith in ourselves. When we do, we put ourselves before Christ and before family. Yet the godly man "greatly delights in His commandments" (Psalm 112:1). He knows God's commandments point out his sin, especially the sin of pride. But he also knows that those commandments were fulfilled by His Savior.

God gave us His commandments to help us see how desperately we need Him. God's Law reflects back to us the hideous truth of our sinful nature and our inability to follow the commandments perfectly. And yet, perfection is what God requires of us in order to live in a right relationship with Him. Because of sin, in this life we cannot be perfect. So, God sent His one and only Son to live a perfect, sinless life for us. And to take away our guilt due to our sins, Jesus died on the cross with all of our sins. Defeating death in the process, now His resurrection declares His victory! Jesus Christ covered our sins with His blood. Now, because of Him, God the Father sees us as His perfect children.

The commandments also guide us in our day-to-day living. We live as Christians in response to God's wonderful gift of grace in His Son. God gives us His Word and His Spirit to help and comfort us through the trials we face each day. As God's Word and Spirit guide us, we become witnesses to those around us. If a picture is worth a thousand words, imagine the impact of your witness as God works through you. Think about how God used godly men in the Bible; think about how God calls men to be the spiritual leader of their families today. He calls us husbands and fathers, employees and citizens, sons and brothers and friends, to do the same. Now that's a heavy load, but the Holy Spirit enables us to fulfill those roles. In so doing, we witness to our loved ones and teach them the importance of including Christ in all that we do.

Writing to Timothy, Paul said,

> Now there is great gain in godliness with contentment, for we brought nothing into the world, and we cannot take anything out of the world. But if we have food and clothing, with these we will be content. But those who desire to be rich fall into temptation, into a snare, into many senseless and harmful desires that plunge people into ruin and destruction. For the love of money is a root of all kinds of evils. It is through this craving that some have wandered away from the faith and pierced themselves with many pangs. But as for you, O man of

God, flee these things. Pursue righteousness, godliness, faith, love, steadfastness, gentleness. Fight the good fight of the faith. Take hold of the eternal life to which you were called and about which you made the good confession in the presence of many witnesses." (1 Timothy 6:6–12)

Paul's words are more than good advice. They impart true spiritual wisdom. That wisdom has its source and its power in "the eternal life to which you were called" (v. 12). Although you have heard it many times, and may have even memorized it as a child, concentrate on what Jesus says to you: "For God so loved the world, that He gave His only Son, that whoever believes in Him should not perish but have eternal life" (John 3:16). Your eternal life is secure in Christ. Through faith in Him, you have become wise. You are in awe of your heavenly Father. So no matter what you are facing, you don't have to be afraid. God, your Savior, is on your side.

....

Your eternal life is secure in Christ. Through faith in Him, you have become wise. You are in awe of your heavenly Father.

Prayer: Dear Lord, thank You for giving me the gift of faith in Your Son. Help me to keep my eyes focused on Jesus, no matter what events surround me. By Your Holy Spirit, grant me the strength I need for each day. I ask this through Christ, our Lord. Amen.

....

Monday

DAILY STUDY QUESTIONS
Psalm 112:1–2

1. The psalm begins with a familiar phrase, or in some translations, a single word: "Praise the LORD," or "Hallelujah!" Is this the exclamation of a believer, or an exhortation to the reader?

2. If the Law always accuses (and it does), how is it possible that one can ever "delight in God's commandments"?

3. What promise does verse 2 offer the faithful father? What part does your "fear of the Lord" play in the fulfillment of this promise?

4. Describe a man who is upright. How does one attain this lofty designation?

Psalm 112:3-4

Wealth and riches are in his house, and his righteousness endures forever. Light dawns in the darkness for the upright; he is gracious, merciful, and righteous.

True Wealth and Riches

We should have been on top of the world. We had just celebrated our son's first birthday. Our daughters, ten and eight, were thriving as we became comfortable in our new surroundings. Let me go back. Two years earlier, my job uprooted us from family and friends in suburban Fairfield County, Connecticut, to the rural farming communities of Southern Illinois. As we prepared for the transition, my daughter, who was six years old at the time, inquired if "people out there spoke English." Transitioning from New England to the Midwest was a real culture shock, but we had turned that corner. Since we moved, the Lord had led us to a wonderful church and school that provided us with a new family and support system.

And yet on that weeknight, my wife and I were sitting in our family room with our pastor. All of a sudden our world was turning upside down. My wife was having a mental and emotional meltdown. What was happening? Why was this happening? How did we get here?

Lord, is this the wealth and riches you promise?

Have you ever wondered what happened to your wealth and riches? If you listen to some televangelists, they will tell you to ask God for that Mercedes-Benz or that million dollar home and it will be yours . . . if you have enough faith. Of course, that flies in the face of what God's Word tells us. God never promises that kind of riches. What we do know from God's Word is that all we have comes from God and that He blesses us in different ways. Paul tells us that we "[have] gifts that differ according to the grace given to us" (Romans 12:6). He also writes, "Blessed be the God and Father of our Lord Jesus Christ, who has blessed us in Christ with every spiritual blessing in the heavenly places" (Ephesians 1:3). Some of the gifts God gives us are physical, while other gifts are spiritual. In His wisdom, God gives us the things we need to accomplish His purposes, not ours. Paul again writes, "Now there are varieties of gifts, but the same Spirit; and there are varieties of service, but the same Lord; and there are varieties of activities, but it is the same God who empowers them all in everyone" (1 Corinthians 12:4–6). When we lose the perspective that all we have comes from God for His purposes, we allow our sinful nature to take over and we begin to focus on ourselves, how we can acquire or keep more possessions, and how much we deserve the things God gives us.

A few weeks ago, while I was walking through a store, a man approached me. He caught me off guard and asked me if I could spare a few dollars so he could get something to eat. My mind was focused on the things that I needed and, without thinking, I said, "Sorry, I can't help you," and he walked away. As I continued down the aisle, I thought to myself, *I ought to go complain to the store manager that they let this guy wander through the store asking people for money,* . . . and then I felt as if the Holy Spirit were knocking on the door to my heart: "Can we talk? Do you remember not so long ago when you and your family did not know where the next meal was coming from?"

My mind quickly went back to that eleven-month period. No job, bill collectors calling—whom do I pay? Do we have enough for groceries? What about the holidays coming up—Thanksgiving, Christmas? It was a difficult time for our family. I felt as if the Holy Spirit were saying, "Remember that?" It was pretty powerful. All I could think of now was *I wonder when this guy last had a meal? I know my belly is full, and I have more than I need, but I still complain at times that I need this or that.* For the next few minutes, I went up and down the aisles looking for this guy to try and give him a few bucks. I lost the opportunity to do with God's gifts what He intends us to do with them: share them.

We all have these life-changing experiences. Sometimes it takes years to gain the perspective necessary for us to see how the Lord blessed us during challenging times. In spite of our short-sightedness, God showers us with His riches, grace, and wisdom. "Light dawns in the darkness for the upright; he is gracious, merciful, and righteous" (Psalm 112:4). God's light—the truth of His love and grace in Christ— rescues us out of those dark times. God also illumines people around us to share that light in word and deed. We are called by God to bring that light to others by sharing the gifts, both physical and spiritual, that He gives us. Jesus tells us in Matthew 5:14–16 that we are "the light of the world" and that we should "let [our] light shine before others, so that they may see your good works and give glory to your Father who is in heaven."

Thanks be to God for His G-R-A-C-E: Gods Riches At Christ's Expense. As Paul reminds us, "For you know the grace of our Lord Jesus Christ, that though He was rich, yet for your sake He became poor, so that you by His poverty might become rich" (2 Corinthians 8:9). There is no greater wealth or riches than the promise of salvation we receive through the blood of our Lord and Savior, Jesus Christ. The riches that He shares with us are immeasurable: His righteousness, grace, and mercy. No one can take this wealth and riches from us. They are ours by grace through faith.

There is no greater wealth or riches than the promise of salvation we receive through the blood of our Lord and Savior, Jesus Christ.

Prayer: Heavenly Father, thank You for all of Your wonderful gifts. Thank You mostly for the riches and wealth of my salvation through Christ, my Lord. Help me to use what You have given me for Your glory and the benefit of others. In Jesus' name. Amen.

Tuesday

DAILY STUDY QUESTIONS
Psalm 112:3-4

1. What wealth and riches fill your home today?

2. How does it feel when the promised wealth of verse 3 doesn't seem to apply to your case? How can life's circumstances both rattle and grow one's faith?

3. How long must one wait for the arrival of light?

4. In what sense is it true that *your* righteousness does endure forever?

Psalm 112:5–6

It is well with the man who deals generously and lends; who conducts his affairs with justice. For the righteous will never be moved; he will be remembered forever.

Be Right to Do Right

Have you ever been to the store and received change for a $20 bill when you gave the cashier a $10 bill? How about this: Have you ever had a basket full of items, and you had a pretty good idea of what the final bill should be, and you were charged $30 or $40 less than what you expected? Then, when you get to your car and review the receipt you realize those jeans you purchased didn't get rung up. Ever find money on the ground? What about a wallet with money inside? I'll bet you've encountered one of those situations before. Now the million-dollar question: what did you do next?

When I was seventeen years old, I thought I was pretty special. Jesus was knocking, but I wasn't listening. It would take another fourteen years before the Holy Spirit worked through God's Word to change my heart. (This is no justification for my actions in the story I am about to tell, but I do hope I would have reacted differently had I been a believer at the time.) I was running with one of my buddies, and for some reason we needed to get in touch with someone by phone. In those days, cell phones were nonexistent. The only thing close to the concept of a cell phone was Captain Kirk's communicator on Star Trek. My buddy and I were on the road so we stopped at the corner store to use the phone booth (remember those?). As we approached it, we noticed a wallet sitting on the shelf in the phone booth. Quickly we made the call and got back in the car. Seeing that no one was around, we thought, *finders keepers, losers weepers*. We opened the wallet and found a hundred-dollar bill. JACKPOT! We split that money and spent it on ourselves.

Just to set the record straight, this was a difficult story to share. It was not one of my shining moments in life, and I am not even sure if I ever told this story to my wife of twenty-five years. She knows now. A couple of years later, on a visit home from college, I went out with some friends. As we headed back to the car at the end of the evening, we were engaging in some testosterone-induced horseplay. I did not

25

realize it then, but during our wrestling match I lost my wallet. When I woke up the next morning, I could not find it. There was not a lot of money, maybe thirty dollars or so, but all of my identification, driver's license, social security card, and college ID were in it. I remembered the wallet I found a few years back and thought I would never see that wallet or anything that was in it again. What a hassle this was going to be to get it replaced. Ironically, three days later I received a package in the mail. It was my wallet with everything intact minus some amount under a dollar that was used to purchase the postage to ship the wallet to me.

As one of its definitions, a dictionary may define *righteous* as "being free from sin or guilt." *Justice* can be defined as "a principle or idea about right conduct." In other words: do the right thing. That surely doesn't fit me. Does it fit you?

Remember the story about the woman who was about to be stoned for adultery? Jesus calmly responded to her accusers, "Let him who is without sin among you be the first to throw a stone at her" (John 8:7). We hear our pastor tells us at the beginning of worship, "If we say we have no sin, we deceive ourselves, and the truth is not in us" (1 John 1:8). How can we "conduct our affairs with justice," as the psalm tells us? If we are not careful, we may fool ourselves into thinking that we have the ability to be generous and just on our own, that we need to do things in order to become righteous before God. The more appropriate question to ask ourselves is not "How can we conduct our affairs with justice?" but only "Can we, apart from God, 'conduct our affairs with justice'?"

In his Letter to the Romans, Paul writes, "For I know that nothing good dwells in me, that is, in my flesh. For I have the desire to do what is right, but not the ability to carry it out" (Romans 7:18). So while we may have the desire to do good, to be just, it takes more than desire to fulfill God's Law. It takes full compliance. That is what God requires for us to be righteous before Him. So where does that leave us? Broken and lost? No! Praise be to God that Jesus Christ, His Son, obeyed every jot and tittle of the Law for us, then shed His blood on Calvary to pay for all the times that we didn't obey the Law. Paul wrote to the Romans, "So by [Jesus'] obedience the many will be made righteous" (Romans 5:19). And to the Corinthians, he said, "In Christ God was reconciling the world to Himself, not counting their trespasses against them" (2 Corinthians 5:19). It is only through our Lord and Savior Jesus Christ and His death and resurrection that we are righteous in God's sight and conduct our affairs with justice.

As a matter of fact, today's psalm verses make more sense if we look at them in reverse. We can "deal generously" and "conduct our affairs with justice" because of the righteousness we have been given through faith in Christ. In other words, before we can "do right," we have to have to "be right" with God. He sets us "free from sin and guilt" through faith in Christ and enables us through faith to "do the right thing." I pray that the person who returned my wallet (minus the dollar) had been enabled to deal generously with me through faith in Christ.

....

We can "deal generously" and "conduct our affairs with justice" because of the righteousness we have been given through faith in Christ.

Prayer: Dear Lord, You desire that all be saved and come to knowledge of Your truth. Help me to do the right thing, not to draw attention to myself, but so that I may be a witness of Your unending love. I ask in Jesus' name. Amen.

....

Wednesday

DAILY STUDY QUESTIONS
Psalm 112:5–6

1. Think of a time when you were not treated justly; how did you react?

2. If justice is rightly defined as giving to each man that which is his legitimate due, what role does justice play in your close relationships?

3. What would complete justice require of you? Think about the past twenty-four hours. Has everything you have done lived up to the standard of full justice?

4. Are there any old acts of injustice that continue to haunt you? How can old sins continue to inflict present pain?

5. Why not confess that old injustice right now? Your Lord is eager to forgive.

Psalm 112:7–8

He is not afraid of bad news; his heart is firm, trusting in the
LORD. His heart is steady; he will not be afraid, until he looks in
triumph on his adversaries.

Good *New* News

"No news is good news."

After twenty-five years working in the computer field, I've grown accustomed to calls coming in at all hours of the night. No matter how many times it happens, though, my heart still races as I awake out of a deep sleep. Once my initial confusion passes and I stop pushing the snooze button on my alarm clock, I realize that the ringing thing is the phone. That's when fear takes hold of me. Who is calling me at this hour? Are all of my kids at home and in bed? Is it Mom or Dad calling to let me know that one or the other has been called home to heaven? Normally, however, it's the office calling to inform me about a computer problem that needs my immediate attention to ensure that the computer systems are operational for the start of business the next day.

What is the worst news that you could get? A pink slip? A diagnosis of a terminal illness for you or a loved one? What about the news of a loved one's or close friend's untimely death? Maybe you have already experienced that type of bad news. No matter how prepared you think you are for such occasions, it is never easy to receive such news. Before such occasions arise, it is helpful to heed Paul's charge: "Put on the whole armor of God, that you may be able to stand against the schemes of the devil" (Ephesians 6:11). The devil loves to work through bad news. Using the difficult situations we face, Satan tries to pull us away from God and His love. The world asks, "How can a loving God allow bad things to happen?" As Christians we know that this question can be answered in one word: sin. Bad things don't happen because God is capricious or cruel; we human beings brought sin—and sin's consequences—into the world. The devil was complicit in that act and now tries to stop us from receiving or leads us to turn us away from the reconciliation that Christ won for us.

Apart from our Lord's unjust suffering and death, the story of Job is perhaps the strongest account of bad things happening to good people. Job "was blameless and upright, one who feared God and turned away from evil" (Job 1:1). Job trusted in God's promises of mercy, and he had profound respect for the Lord. He also sought to follow the Lord's ways. However, Job, who was blessed with wealth and a large family, lost it all. How did he react? "In all this Job did not sin or charge God with wrong" (Job 1:22). Although Job remained faithful, he felt that God owed him an explanation for the trials that he went through. Job prayed to God and asked, "Why?" Finally, God spoke to Job and asked him, "Where were you when I laid the foundation of the earth?" (Job 38:4). It was then that Job realized that God is God, and that God did not owe him any explanation. Job confessed and repented, "I had heard of You by the hearing of the ear, but now my eye sees You; therefore I despise myself, and repent in dust and ashes" (Job 42:5–6). In the end, God blessed Job. "And the LORD restored the fortunes of Job, when he had prayed for his friends. And the LORD gave Job twice as much as he had before" (Job 42:10).

When bad news arrives, it doesn't come empty-handed. It comes carrying baggage—baggage like pain, suffering, and loss. Sometimes the baggage is physical, sometimes it is emotional, and many times it is both. I know that suffering is not high on my list of things I want out of life, but God has a different plan for you and me. He tells us, "Trust in the LORD with all your heart, and do not lean on your own understanding" (Proverbs 3:5). Trusting in the Lord, our hearts are firm in Him. It is through Him that we can endure the hurt that bad news brings. And God also strengthens us as Christians through those trials and sufferings. The apostle Paul tells us, "More than that, we rejoice in our sufferings, knowing that suffering produces endurance, and endurance produces character, and character produces hope, and hope does not put us to shame, because God's love has been poured into our hearts through the Holy Spirit who has been given to us" (Romans 5:3–5).

Men, always remember that Christ triumphed over all of our adversaries—sin, Satan, hell, and death—when He died on the cross. The writer to the Hebrews puts it this way, "[Jesus] Himself likewise partook of [flesh and blood], that through death He might destroy the one who has the power of death, that is, the devil, and deliver all those who through fear of death were subject to lifelong slavery" (2:14–15).

Jesus was also raised in resurrection victory! Should we look forward to bad news? My vote is no, but I do know that we can trust in God and His promises. "Even though I walk through the valley of the shadow of death, I will fear no evil, for You are with me; Your rod and Your staff, they comfort me" (Psalm 23:4). "The sting of death is sin, and the power of sin is the law. But thanks be to God, who gives us the victory through our Lord Jesus Christ" (1 Corinthians 15:56–57).

Brothers, bad news is a part of this fallen world we live in. But even in the midst of bad news, there is other news, and this news is good! God really does love everyone in the world, and He proved His love by sending His Son to die for our sins on the cross. All who believe in Him have eternal life. That's the kind of news that will keep you, your family, and friends firm and secure, whatever you or they may face. It's the Good News that's always new!

Brothers, bad news is a part of this fallen world we live in. But even in the midst of bad news, there is other news, and this news is good!

Prayer: Dear God, strengthen my faith so that when I receive bad news, my heart is firm in the promises of Your Word and my confidence is fixed on the Good News of Your Son, Jesus Christ. In His name I pray. Amen.

Thursday

DAILY STUDY QUESTIONS
Psalm 112:7–8

1. Think of a time that you experienced unexpected bad news. How did you feel? How did you respond?

2. Is a strong reaction to bad news a sign of a heart that does not trust in the Lord? If someone breaks down, does it mean that he or she has a deficient or immature faith?

3. In what ways might it be true that a stolid, stoical response to bad news is a poor witness to one's faith in God?

4. What's the difference between actually getting bad news and living in fear of receiving bad news?

5. What would it mean for you to look in triumph on your adversaries?

Psalm 112:9–10

He has distributed freely; he has given to the poor; his
righteousness endures forever; his horn is exalted in honor.
The wicked man sees it and is angry; he gnashes his teeth and
melts away; the desire of the wicked will perish!

Forever and Ever

Our psalm this week has focused on the comfort Christians have as they seek to serve God and their fellow man. Christians aren't impervious to being hurt; the devil, the world, and our sinful flesh wage war against us. In spite of these woes, the man righteous by faith in Christ "has distributed freely; he has given to the poor; his righteousness endures forever." His righteousness endures forever because the good deeds he has accomplished have been done in repentant faith.

Have you ever thought about how long is forever? Forever is a pretty long time. Remember when you were a kid and you couldn't wait for Christmas to arrive? It seemed like that day would take forever to get here—and you were thinking that on the day after Thanksgiving! As we get older (and wiser, we hope), *forever* takes on a whole new meaning. Now we need forever to meet all of our work and family commitments. How can we ever get it all done?

Forever really is a foreign concept to us sinful human beings. When God spoke the universe into being, He also created time. "And God said, 'Let there be light,' and there was light. And God saw that the light was good. And God separated the light from the darkness. God called the light Day, and the darkness He called Night. And there was evening and there was morning, the first day" (Genesis 1:3–5). Because you and I are created in and are bound by time, forever is impossible to imagine. God understands time because He created it; He also understands the concept of forever, because He stands outside time. Indeed, there are many mysteries when it comes to the things of God.

In the Book of Isaiah, God tells us "For as the heavens are higher than the earth, so are My ways higher than your ways and My thoughts than your thoughts" (Isaiah 55:9). From the beginning of time, man has had trouble accepting that fact—starting with Adam and Eve, to the tower of Babel, to Moses, to David, to Peter, to you and to me. As Christians, we wrestle with the old Adam, our inborn, sinful nature. That nature wars against us to keep us from knowing and understanding the things of God. You would think that God would have run out of patience with us a long time ago. But as God's Word tells us, "As far as the east is from the west, so far does He remove our transgressions from us" (Psalm 103:12). God's forgiveness through Jesus Christ is so complete, it is radical.

That is another awesome thing we may have trouble wrapping our natural minds around. Have you ever really considered how far the east is from the west? Why would God use east and west? Think of a number line that goes off in two opposite directions. If you start a journey in one direction (say, east) and continue on that plane, you will never reach the other direction (west). You can even travel forever, and you'll never reach your destination. That's how far Jesus Christ took our sins away from us when he died on the cross. Wow! How can we be worthy of that? The answer is we can't be worthy. There is nothing we can do to gain that righteousness. That is why Christ had to take all of our sins to the cross and why we call the Gospel the Good News. The Book of Isaiah tells us "all our righteous deeds are like a polluted garment" (Isaiah 64:6). The righteousness that we have comes only from our faith in Christ, which is God's gift to us by the Holy Spirit through God's Word.

Now, we do respond to God's Word and the Gospel message with the assistance and guidance of the Holy Spirit. God instructs us through His Word, "You shall not harden your heart or shut your hand against your poor brother, but you shall open your hand to him and lend him sufficient for his need, whatever it may be" (Deuteronomy 15:7–8). Jesus spoke often of servanthood and, along with that servanthood, humility. Jesus said, "Whoever exalts himself will be humbled, and whoever humbles himself will be exalted" (Matthew 23:12). Throughout the Bible, we read about great men and women of the faith who endured all sorts of trials and tribulations while being strengthened by the Lord and His grace. The writer to the Hebrews extols these saints:

> These all died in faith, not having received the things promised, but having seen them and greeted them from afar, and having acknowledged that they were strangers and exiles on the earth. For people who speak thus make it clear that they are seeking a homeland. If they had been thinking of that land from which they had gone out, they would have had opportunity to return. But as it is, they desire a better country, that is, a heavenly one. Therefore God is not ashamed to be called their God, for He has prepared for them a city. (Hebrews 11:13–16)

Jesus reminds us, "Do not lay up for yourselves treasures on earth, where moth and rust destroy and where thieves break in and steal, but lay up for yourselves treasures in heaven, where neither moth nor rust destroys and where thieves do not break in and steal. For where your treasure is, there your heart will be also" (Matthew 6:19–21).

The world chases its dreams here in time on earth, searching for fulfillment, fame, and fortune. The world will only be disappointed. We Christians, however, respond to God's free gift of salvation in Christ by the deeds we do for eternity. Acceptable to God for Christ's sake because they are done in repentant faith, our good deeds will last forever. *Forever* and *forgiven* are strange words to the natural man. But to the man blessed by God, the key to understanding them is faith.

....

We Christians, however, respond to God's free gift of salvation in Christ by the deeds we do for eternity.

Prayer: Lord Jesus, thank You for sending Your Holy Spirit, who helps me to understand Your Word. Help me to apply what He teaches me so that I may lay up true treasures in heaven. I ask in Your name. Amen.

....

Friday

DAILY STUDY QUESTIONS
Psalm 112:9-10

1. How righteous do you feel today?

2. What does giving freely to the poor have to do with one's righteousness?

3. How is it possible that *your* righteousness will endure forever?

4. While God's Righteous One will be exalted and blessed eternally, the wicked will not fare so well. How do you react to the graphic description of the wicked?

5. What do you think is the purpose of verse 10?

Week One

PSALM 112

The 112th psalm is a psalm of comfort in which the pious, who fear God, are praised for their good life and are promised eternal comfort against all trouble. They are especially commended to a sincere confidence and trust in God's grace, so that they may be undismayed and undaunted (which is the real, true faith) until they see the destruction of the godless and their foes.

– Martin Luther

GROUP BIBLE STUDY
(Questions and answers on pp. 164–66.)

1. What do you think of when you hear the word *righteous*? What does it mean to be righteous?

2. Describe the most righteous man you have ever known. What was his most compelling quality or characteristic?

3. Is there a difference between being blessed and being righteous? Using the descriptions in the psalm, describe the characteristics of a man who is blessed and righteous.

4. Verse 1 declares that the first two criteria of blessedness are fear of the Lord and delight in His commandments. What does it mean to "fear the Lord"? How do these ideas fit with a Christian perspective?

5. The psalm counts children as one of the marks of God's blessing. What is the correlation between a man's righteousness (the righteousness he achieves by his faithful living) and the success of his heirs? What is the definition or mark of a successful child?

6. Consider verse 4. In what tangible ways does God bring His light into the darkness?

7. The old saying "neither a borrower nor a lender be" seems to contradict the exhortation of verse 5. What is the value in being willing to lend? Why are we often reluctant to follow the psalmist's urging?

8. Jesus concurred with the words of verse 7 when He commanded us not to worry (Matthew 6:25–34)—not when receiving bad news and not when dreading bad news. What things might tempt a man to worry? How does a heart steadfast in the Lord aid in overcoming worry and fear?

9. Are verses 8 and 13 being somehow vindictive with their emphasis on looking with satisfaction on one's adversaries or enemies? How should a Christian understand this idea?

10. Think about the psalm's description of a righteous man and name one thing that you will do this week to help you live righteously in one of those areas.

Week Two

Psalm 119:1-8

[1] Blessed are those whose way is blameless,
who walk in the law of the LORD!

[2] Blessed are those who keep His testimonies,
who seek Him with their whole heart,

[3] who also do no wrong,
but walk in His ways!

[4] You have commanded Your precepts
to be kept diligently.

[5] Oh that my ways may be steadfast
in keeping Your statutes!

[6] Then I shall not be put to shame,
having my eyes fixed on all Your commandments.

[7] I will praise You with an upright heart,
when I learn your righteous rules.

[8] I will keep Your statutes;
do not utterly forsake me!

John Crowe

Psalm 119:1

Blessed are those whose way is blameless, who walk in the
law of the LORD!

Blameless and Blessed

What does it mean to walk blamelessly, to follow a blameless path in the ways of the Lord? Some days that seems like a daunting—if not impossible—task. Imagine living a life that is only dreamed and never accomplished. Therein lies the beauty of Psalm 119: the psalmist couples the Law's demands for utter perfection and its power to convict us of sin with the blessings of following God and His way. Walking in God's Word, His laws, precepts, statutes, commands, decrees, way(s), and His promises as described throughout Scripture is God's blessing and gift to us. How do we know? Christ has restored us (Galatians 4:4–5) to a right relationship with God and His holy, righteous, and good Law (Romans 3:19–23).

When we think about keeping laws, statutes, commands, and so on, the word *discipline* comes to mind. Many things we do in this life as men require discipline, and require it in abundance. Discipline is a real blessing from the Lord when it is observed in the light of His grace and forgiveness. Take a highly skill-oriented sport like tennis, for example. Having played competitive tennis for quite a few years, one of my favorite things to do is to teach people (especially children) how to excel at tennis. Once, when I was between corporate jobs, I took the time to get my professional teaching certification so that I could put some credentials behind my lifelong love of the sport. In tennis, one must be incredibly disciplined in shot execution and in a variety of shot choices. In each shot in each point of a game, it is much more about strategy than execution. When a competitive player reaches the point where shot execution comes quite naturally and at a high level of consistency, he or she then enters into a whole new level of the game. Getting to that level requires countless hours of work and hitting thousands and thousands of tennis balls. From a human standpoint, this is achievable with work, time, and discipline. Yet, even then, it does not guarantee that the player will be the next Roger Federer or Maria Sharapova.

At this point, you might be asking yourself, What does playing competitive tennis have to do with keeping God's laws? The point that I'm making is really quite simple. Regardless of what we do, say, promote, strive for, dream about, and so on, we'll never be perfect at it. And yet, God continues to hand out His gifts of life to us through Christ's perfect life for us and His sacrifice for our sins.

We men work very hard at trying to accomplish a long list of objectives. If only we could get that promotion faster, that corner office sooner, or that "C-level" title, then life would be fulfilling and we would have "arrived." As Christians, it's sometimes easy to think that because we are righteous before God by what we do that God will somehow let us more easily attain our earthly goals and get ahead of the next guy. Nice idea, but definitely not what God has in mind. Jesus makes that very clear: "And when [Jesus] was in the house He asked them, 'What were you discussing on the way?' But they kept silent, for on the way they had argued with one another about who was the greatest. And He sat down and called the twelve. And He said to them, 'If anyone would be first, he must be last of all and servant of all'" (Mark 9:33–35). The great privilege of our Christian life is serving others because of the hope and gift of Christ for us. Indeed, even when it even comes to "our" achievements, it is *He* that lives in and through us.

Going back to the tennis analogy, becoming a disciplined machine at hitting serves, volleys, forehands, backhands, overheads, topspin lobs, and so on will not guarantee that one will win Wimbledon or the U.S. Open. In the same way, even the most faithful follower of God's wonderful plan for us to "walk in *His* ways" has no guarantee of an easy, achievement-filled life. In spite of our sin and disobedience, God loves us so much that He sent Jesus to the cross to earn our forgiveness. Our righteousness before God comes by faith in Christ, not by what we do (Romans 3:22). Indeed, we were baptized into Christ's righteousness (Galatians 3:27), His perfect fulfilling of God's laws for us. Because of Jesus, when God looks at us as Christians, instead of seeing our failures, sins, and self-centered striving for personal glory, He only sees Jesus. At times we may think we have done everything perfectly, that we have made certain accomplishments. We can become quite full of ourselves. But God makes the story of our success not about us at all, but all about Jesus and what He achieved for us by His life, death, and resurrection. Put another way, as Christians, we have gotten it all through Christ even though we've done nothing to deserve it or earn it.

What a gift to be blessed by the Lord and seen as blameless in His sight! As we live our lives concentrating on His story, may we remember today that the discipline of God's Law shows our continual need for Jesus, "the founder and perfecter of our faith" (Hebrews 12:2). The accomplishments, titles, and awards we achieve are put in a right perspective when viewed in the light of Jesus and His saving grace. Jesus makes our way and our walk blameless, and we are blessed. As you face today, keep His Word on your mind: "For by grace you have been saved through faith. And this is not of your own doing; it is the gift of God, not a result of works, so that no one may boast. For we are His workmanship, created in Christ Jesus for good works, which God prepared beforehand, that we should walk in them" (Ephesians 2:8–10). Truly "blessed are those whose way is blameless, who walk in the law of the LORD!" (Psalm 119:1).

The accomplishments, titles, and awards we achieve are put in a right perspective when viewed in the light of Jesus and His saving grace.

Prayer: Lord Jesus Christ, thank You for walking the perfect way of Your Father's Law for me. Through Your Word, help me to be disciplined in what I think, say, and do, so that I might bring glory and honor to Your name. Amen.

Monday

DAILY STUDY QUESTIONS
Psalm 119:1

1. *Blameless* is not a word we hear much in daily vocabulary. Why is this? What does it mean to be blameless?

2. What is the difference between walking in the Law and being an expert in the Law?

3. Can a man's walk in God's Law improve with practice? Is such walking a one-time choice that norms all subsequent life, or is it a daily process?

4. Since no one can be perfect, is being blameless just an ideal (meant to show us our sin) or a reality for which we should strive?

5. What areas of your walk need the most practice so that you can more nearly walk as one who is blameless?

Psalm 119:2-3

Blessed are those who keep His testimonies, who seek Him
with their whole heart, who also do no wrong, but walk in His
ways!

In the Spotlight

How does a man seek something with his whole heart? There are many things
we can seek after or strive for in this world, but how can we daily put our entire being into seeking after God's testimonies? One of the many blessings of Baptism is
that the Spirit of God takes up residence in our hearts and dwells within us (1 Corinthians 12:13). Christ truly is with us and in us. As Paul said, "It is no longer I who
live, but Christ who lives in me" (Galatians 2:20). Jesus enables us to keep God's
testimonies and to seek God's statutes with our whole heart.

When Jesus told Nicodemus, "Unless one is born of water and the Spirit, he
cannot enter the kingdom of God" (John 3:5), He was talking about being born
again through Baptism. But what does that mean in a "practical" sense? How does
that tie into what I do? How can I live out my life as a mature Christian and not
just as a spiritual infant? How can I, as a Christian man, seek God with my whole
heart?

As a young man, I had a great desire to be a musical entertainer. Some early suc-
cesses as a teenager in auditions, talent contests, school events and the like encouraged me to consider a life in show business. As I headed off to university, I dreamed
about being in front of big crowds doing what I loved best: performing. God certainly had other plans for me, plans that I had not much considered until I was in college
and became fully engaged with the "show and travel" life. As an eighteen-year-old,
I performed with a live musical dance and review show that required that I travel to
multiple states two or three times per week. After about one "glamorous" month, I
met some performers who were struggling with more than I could imagine, given my
simple Midwestern small-town upbringing. One (probably the most talented vocal-
ist) was addicted to cocaine, another already had a serious alcohol problem, and yet
another was totally broke and had lost every bit of support from her family. Just a
few social gatherings, looking more like private pharmacies than anything, caused

me to reevaluate the direction of my life. It seemed that everyone I met was more self-centered than God- or others-centered.

Ironically, the more talented the dancers or promising young musicians were, the more self-absorbed they seemed to be. Quite literally, the greater the applause, promotion, status, visibility, and so on, the greater the degree of despair and loneliness. For most, consuming all of their energy seeking approval led to disastrous consequences in their young lives. There were a few bright spots where folks had managed to buck the trend, but it looked like that would be an incredibly difficult feat given the demands and the busy schedules we had with our travels and studies. What a difficult environment for a young Christian to live a godly and humble life according to Scripture.

We humans have some freedom to choose what is good, right, true, just, and beautiful and to do things subject to human reason. However, if we trust in them for eternal life, we are doomed for failure, even while the world (and our lying hearts) claim success. Paul says, "What becomes of our boasting? It is excluded. By what kind of law? By a law of works? No, but by the law of faith. For we hold that one is justified by faith apart from works of the law" (Romans 3:27–28). So, even seeking God out with our whole hearts means nothing when it comes to our salvation. Our seeking means something only in the light of the Gospel's saving grace. God plunged our attention-seeking flesh into Baptism's water, and out of that water He gave us new birth by water and the Spirit. We now are part of His eternal kingdom.

Clearly, this means we need not remain spiritual infants, but we can mature into "new men." Through God's Word, the same Spirit enables us to seek after God with our (actually Jesus') whole heart. God declares us righteous through faith in Christ; then with Christ dwelling within us, He enables us to become righteous. All attention is focused on Him, not on us.

So what about show business? Well, after three months or so on the road, I decided that there was probably a better way to spend my life. I transferred to another university and still was very active in music but in a way that I could center the music in my life on service to others and to the Church. The glimmer and glamour of the spotlight was still enticing, but even at eighteen, I knew that my chances were much better if I stayed away from life on the road. That, coupled with getting to be much closer to the love of my life (now my beautiful wife of twenty-five years), made it easy to walk in a new direction. I pursued a business career and have worked in business vocations now for over twenty years, including my current position working for a church and school.

So how do men seek after God's own heart? Quite simply, through the power of the Holy Spirit working through God's Word. Christ, who is alive in us and working through us, changes our heart to one like His. Forgiving us even when we fail to put God first in our lives, through His covenant of grace, He enables us to live as godly men in His sight. Walking in God's "ways" (Psalm 119:3) is something that He does with and through us. What a joy and relief that it isn't on our shoulders to seek God on our own but that God seeks and calls us out to us through Christ.

So how do men seek after God's own heart? Quite simply, through the power of the Holy Spirit working through God's Word.

Prayer: Heavenly Father, forgive me for the times I have wanted the spotlight to shine on me. Through the Gospel and the Sacraments, stir up Your Spirit within me so that I may seek You with my whole heart and walk in Your ways. In Jesus' name. Amen.

Tuesday

DAILY STUDY QUESTIONS
Psalm 119:2-3

1. What unique images does the idea of God's testimonies conjure in your mind?

2. How do these psalm verses challenge the notion that one may be a casual follower of Jesus—one who may fit into the culture without much difficulty?

3. How sincere (or wholehearted) is sincere enough?

4. Should a man do God's will or His testimony even if he is not completely pure or sincere in his motivations?

5. If true righteousness is found only in Christ's forgiveness, what kind of righteousness am I supposed to be pursuing in my life?

Psalm 119:4–5

You have commanded Your precepts to be kept diligently.
Oh that my ways may be steadfast in keeping Your statutes!

No Need for Do-Overs

Is there anything absolute? Is there a right and wrong? Is there truth that never changes, is never altered, and is unconditional? These questions are asked and answered every day in our universities and in our daily lives. In a post-modern society, truth is whatever satisfies your desires or wishes at the moment. You are told you can make something true merely by either saying that it is or by molding words and phrases into a shape that fits your desires. As Christian men living in this kind of society, it is very important that we clearly understand the simple and absolute truths of God's Word. This will keep us focused on our Lord, instead of trying to explain everything by humanistic relativism. Everything changes when we embrace God's truth, the Word, specifically Jesus and His Gospel, as the final revelation of God's saving will.

We live in a world that is excuse rich. Everything from "we just ran out of time" to "we just scheduled too much that weekend" to the proverbial "the dog ate my homework" permeates our speech and our hearing. With so many activities on our plate, we have perfected the ability of quickly creating the next three reasons why we failed to keep our word, broke a commitment, or reneged on a promise we made to our wives or children. The world is a place chock full of cover-ups, weak excuses, and the infamous do-overs that we invoked in our childhood.

Do-overs are my favorite. I enjoyed playing sports as a youngster (still do), and always took great exception to the number of times a do-over was called by the opposing side. Some kids mastered the do-over. They used it when they struck out at Wiffle ball, threw a gutter ball in bowling, double-faulted in tennis, were distracted by a barking dog while shooting a free throw in the driveway, or failed to get the kickoff in football past the corner of the house.

One do-over that I have enjoyed in adult life is the infamous mulligan in a friendly game of golf. How could anyone refuse this wonderful gift after slicing a tee shot into the pond to the right, the house to the left, or simply short of the women's tee? Probably the most interesting example of those are when you play in the church golf outing (scramble) and you actually can purchase mulligans—usually for $5 or $10 each to go to the cause that the outing is fund-raising for. What a concept: pay for the right to make excuses later on because you know you'll mess up. Sounds sort of like a misguided theological debate . . . but more on that later.

Isn't it great to know that as Christians all we need to do is take God at His Word, and all of the stress, confusion, and guilt of making excuses simply do not matter? We never need be afraid or confused about our salvation and what the Lord has done for us. Instead of viewing God's laws as things that sound good on days they fit our agenda, God's grace allows us to embrace the freedom that Christ purchased and won for us on the cross, and to begin doing the good works He has prepared in advance for us to do (Ephesians 2:10). Yes, God's grace even leads us earnestly to ask that our ways may be steadfast in keeping His statutes.

Jesus is "the way, and the truth, and the life. No one comes to the Father except through [Him]" (John 14:6). What a privilege of confessing our sins and then being forgiven because of Him. Jesus is the ultimate excuse breaker. As God, Jesus is the Lawgiver. And yet, He is also the Law Fulfiller (Matthew 5:17). What an amazing grace that our God works for our salvation! Another parallel of this is found in John's Gospel: "And as Moses lifted up the serpent in the wilderness, so must the Son of Man be lifted up, that whoever believes in Him may have eternal life" (John 3:14–15). The truth here is that because the Israelites grumbled in the wilderness, God punished them with poisonous snakes. However, God also provided an antidote by telling Moses to make a bronze serpent and to put it on a pole for the Israelites to see. By gazing upon it, the people would be healed. Remember the snake in the Garden of Eden? Likewise, Moses' snake represented sin and the fall in the garden. Yet Jesus says that Moses' snake pointed forward to the time when Jesus would hang on the cross and die for all our sins. Paul says, "Christ redeemed us from the curse of the law by becoming a curse for us—for it is written, 'Cursed is everyone who is hung on a tree'" (Galatians 3:13). And Peter writes that Jesus "bore our sins in His body on the tree, that we might die to sin and live to righteousness" (1 Peter 2:24). The Lawgiver was born under the Law to take the place of the lawless. Sinless Jesus took on our sin to take our sin away.

In a world that is excuse ridden, what a blessing and a joy for us to know that our "ways may be steadfast in keeping [God's] statutes" (Psalm 119:5) through the redemption we have received from Jesus Christ. As our postmodern world tries to find meaning in relativism, may we delight in God's Law, perfectly fulfilled by our

Savior. Because He is the truth made flesh, there's no need for do-overs. Instead, like the psalmist, we pray that He will help us keep His statues diligently.

In a world that is excuse ridden, what a blessing and a joy for us to know that our "ways may be steadfast in keeping [God's] statutes" (Psalm 119:5).

Prayer: Dear God, forgive me for making excuses to You, my wife, my kids, my employer, and my friends. Help me to follow Jesus, so that I may keep Your commandments to the glory of Your name. For Jesus' sake. Amen.

Wednesday

DAILY STUDY QUESTIONS
Psalm 119:4–5

1. Looking back over the last week, was there a time when you would dearly love to be able to purchase a life mulligan and do it over again?

2. Think of a time when a rule or practice changed without warning and left you in a tight spot. What's wrong with arbitrary rules and rule makers?

3. Statutes and commandments don't bend. How is that both convicting and comforting?

4. In what ways is God's intervention in Christ an unexpected surprise?

5. In what ways is forgiveness in Christ is better than having the ability to call a do-over when your actions don't measure up?

Psalm 119:6–7

Then I shall not be put to shame, having my eyes fixed
on all Your commandments. I will praise You with an upright
heart, when I learn Your righteous rules.

No More Shame

Do you think there is a sense of shame anymore? It seems that in many circles there is no shame at all. Why is this so? When godly men experience shame, they need only confess their sins and remember the shame Jesus experienced for us on the cross. Today, one is more likely to be shamed by his peers for lack of tolerance or inclusiveness than for serious moral matters that years ago would have caused more than a blush. In a world where everything is relative, why be ashamed about anything? With a bit of logic or by frankly applying some situational ethics, everything is okay. "I'm okay, and you're okay," right? Well, maybe not. Listen to Paul: "See to it that no one takes you captive by philosophy and empty deceit, according to human tradition, according to the elemental spirits of the world, and not according to Christ" (Colossians 2:8).

I have memories, some fond, some not so much, of my mother, grandmother, and aunts telling us children "shame on you," "you ought to be ashamed of yourself," or as they say in the South, "for shame, for shame." Of course, we heard those things after we had either gotten ourselves in trouble or were caught by surprise before our plots had fully hatched.

My family of origin had a lot of rules. Perhaps yours did too. It seemed that everything and everyone in my family was affected by "the rules." Do this, don't do that, and so on. In my family, those rules purportedly came straight from biblical teaching. To be sure, children need structure and the protection rules offer, otherwise there would be fewer teenagers walking around on earth. (Perhaps teenagers need even more rules.) And as Christian adults, we need to follow the rules too. But children don't usually understand the meaning or purpose of rules. Even Christian adults fail sometimes to see the real beauty God's rules, His statutes and commandments. God's rules are true. They are perfect. And they are just. Unlike the rules and regulations I grew up with, God's rule, His Law, never changes.

To be sure, the Law convicts us of our sins. When we were caught by our moms or grandmothers or aunts doing something we shouldn't have been doing, we were (hopefully) ashamed. The same thing holds true today. Standing before a righteous God whose Law declares us guilty, we're embarrassed. Caught red handed. Guilty. But, John says, "the blood of Jesus [God's] Son cleanses us from all sin" (1 John 1:7). The God who condemns is also the God who forgives. The God who demands perfection freely bestows perfection. The God of the Law is also the God of the Gospel. Having satisfied His righteous judgment on His Son on the cross, God sets us scot-free.

It's simply amazing to ponder that all mankind fell when Adam broke God's Word, but that God restored all mankind through Jesus, the Word made flesh.

> "Therefore, as one trespass led to condemnation for all men, so one act of righteousness leads to justification and life for all men. For as by the one man's disobedience the many were made sinners, so by the one man's obedience the many will be made righteous. Now the law came in to increase the trespass, but where sin increased, grace abounded all the more, so that, as sin reigned in death, grace also might reign through righteousness leading to eternal life through Jesus Christ our Lord." (Romans 5:18–21)

As godly men, then, we are motivated and enabled to follow God's Law because the Word made flesh gives us eternal life and righteousness. Our response to God's great work for us by sending Jesus is the privilege of keeping His Word. Since we died with Christ in our Baptism, we also live with Him as He lives in us as His resurrection people. "Do not present your members to sin as instruments for unrighteousness, but present yourselves to God as those who have been brought from death to life, and your members to God as instruments for righteousness. For sin will have no dominion over you, since you are not under law but under grace" (Romans 6:13–14). When we are truly under grace, we can't help but seek God's Law with all of our heart. A concept frequently misunderstood by Christians is that God doesn't save us only to expect us to do good for others or for Him by relying on ourselves. Why would He need that if He's truly God? Rather, we emulate the good works of Jesus, the Suffering Servant, because of the grace freely given to us. We have the privilege of doing good works for others and the Church because of the gift of grace, not because we "have to" do them to stay in God's good graces. So much false shame goes into that kind of wrong thinking. Doing good works is a response to God's gift of grace. We do good to others because of what Jesus has done for us. We expect nothing in return in this world. We are, in effect, being Jesus for others in how we act and interact with them. Better said, Jesus is loving and caring for others through us.

Even though the phrase "shame on you" has all but vanished, and that could be both good and bad, the blessing that we have as Christians is that our shame and guilt were all washed away by the cleansing blood of Christ. Jesus kept God's laws perfectly for us, and now no one can accuse us, not even the devil. Jesus is our substitute and Savior. Because of that, we strive to keep His Word in humility. "With my whole heart I seek You; let me not wander from Your commandments! I have stored up Your word in my heart, that I might not sin against You" (Psalm 119:10–11).

> The blessing that we have as Christians is that our shame and guilt were all washed away by the cleansing blood of Christ.
>
> *Prayer: Blessed Holy Spirit, renew a right spirit within me. Confront me with Your Law, but take away my sin through the blood of My Savior. Keep my eyes fixed on Him, who obeyed the commandments perfectly for me. I ask in Jesus' name. Amen.*

Thursday

DAILY STUDY QUESTIONS
Psalm 119:6-7

1. Think of a time recently when you felt the flushed, red-faced discomfort of shame. What prompted it? Was the shame appropriate?

2. Is shame always a wrong or illegitimate feeling? When might it be a good thing for a man to feel shame?

3. What would it mean to be able to look at the Ten Commandments and feel no shame?

4. How does this way of looking at the Law differ from the idea that the purpose of the Law is simply to expose sin and convict sinners?

5. When was the last time you thanked God for teaching you about His righteous judgments, that is, His will, His Law? Why doesn't this happen more often?

Psalm 119:8

I will keep Your statutes; do not utterly forsake me!

Christ Is with Us

Life in this world presents challenges, joys, sorrows, and blessings. While we go through our daily adventures, the support of family, friends, and colleagues is a great blessing. In addition, we have Jesus, who promises never to leave us. Seeking His will in His Word, we can be assured of finding ways that are righteous. When we fail, He promises rich forgiveness. His Spirit dwells in our hearts. His Word challenges and comforts us, His promises in Baptism never leave us, and His Supper nourishes us. His gracious presence provides the true support and sustenance we need to walk in His ways.

Psalm 119 is such a rich psalm; take some time to read the whole thing. It points out not only the beauty and power of God's laws and statutes but also the comfort and reassurance we have in knowing that God is mercifully with us. In the latter part of this psalm, you read the familiar "Your Word is a lamp to my feet and a light to my path," (v. 105) and, "But You are near, O Lord, and all Your commandments are true" (v. 151). In these verses, the psalmist praises God for the reassurance we have, knowing that He guides our ways and does so with the completeness of His truth. The most reassuring hope, though, is contained in verses 41–43: "Let Your steadfast love come to me, O Lord, Your salvation according to Your promise; then shall I have an answer for him who taunts me, for I trust in Your word. And take not the word of truth utterly out of my mouth, for my hope is in Your rules." God's promise of salvation, His sending Jesus to die on the cross for our sins, is the ultimate assurance that He is always with us. At our Baptism, we received God's Holy Spirit to guide us into all truth. He is the mark, the sign, and the seal of Jesus in our hearts.

Jesus, then, is with us all of the time—and not just in the sense of being some kind of a deflector shield, or a defensive weapon to strike down all of the external evil things that come at us. Rather, our Lord is a permanent resident in our lives and our being, He lives in our very hearts and souls.

The second of my five children, a teenager, is a master at video games. Although I'm quite sure this great skill won't help him get into any Ivy League schools or make him a millionaire, it seems to be a good way for him to relax. His favorite games are any that have knights, soldiers, battles, or the like. In the world of electronic conflicts, he is always armed with some sort of weapon, be it a sword, gun, or lightsaber. But when he, or rather his game character, is most powerful is when his play has been rewarded with extra abilities. These abilities are sometimes called "health," "wealth," or "extra energy." They are usually invisible and cannot be used unless needed. He can draw on them when the battle is not going so well or merely if he wants to get a good start at a particular level. Sometimes I wish video games had never been invented for all of the new distractions and mind-numbing hours they have brought to my home.

However, I've learned that video games are good for observing how human beings interact and for determining what they value. Every time my son (who is quite skilled at these games) goes into battle or plays even the simplest games, he is always more concerned about security and assurance of the extra abilities or force that he can take into battle than just his skill as a swordsman, or whatever. When I asked him why that these extra abilities were so important to him, he said something very interesting. He said, "You know, Dad, whenever you enter a difficult situation in the world, you have a much better chance of prevailing when you have a built-in edge or backup plan that will never fail." Much like my son's video game analogy, having Jesus with you all of the time means not having to worry about what will happen—regardless how everything turns out.

Men, Christ is with us. We know that for a fact, because His Word says so. Because Jesus is with us, proven through His promises in Baptism and the Lord's Supper, we have the ultimate support system available. In fact, with Jesus working in us a as we are obedient to His Word, He is actually doing His work through us. As we live according to His Word, others see Christ in us. Jesus said, "You are the light of the world. A city set on a hill cannot be hidden. Nor do people light a lamp and put it under a basket, but on a stand, and it gives light to all in the house. In the same way, let your light shine before others, so that they may see your good works and give glory to your Father who is in heaven" (Matthew 5:14–16). With Christ, the light of the world, in us and with us every day, we are comforted and others may come to know Him.

A man's way is truly blameless, then, when the saving grace of our Lord Jesus Christ is upon him. We don't need our own special powers to resolve all the problems of the world. Rather, our Lord allows us to use our created gifts to solve problems and we are never alone in this endeavor. We look to God's Word, especially the words and person of our Lord Jesus Christ. God has given us His Son and the indwelling presence of His Holy Spirit. May the psalmist's focus be ours at the end of this week, "The LORD is my portion; I promise to keep Your words. I entreat Your favor with all my heart; be gracious to me according to Your promise" (Psalm 119:57–58).

....

We don't need our own special powers to resolve all the problems of the world. Rather, our Lord allows us to use our created gifts to solve problems and we are never alone in this endeavor.

Prayer: Heavenly Father, thank You for the support of family, friends, and colleagues in my life. Thank You mostly for Jesus, who is always with me. In His name I pray. Amen.

....

Friday

DAILY STUDY QUESTIONS
Psalm 119:8

1. What would life be like if God did forsake you utterly?

2. Is the psalmist saying that *because* he is keeping God's Law or statutes he can therefore implore God not to forsake him?

3. How can you be sure that God will not forsake you?

4. In truth, only one human being has ever been forsaken by God. When did this happen (see Matthew 27:46)?

5. What difference does Jesus' work make when it comes to your striving to keep God's commandments?

Week Two

PSALM 119

The 119th psalm is a long psalm, containing prayers, comforts, instructions, and thanks in great number. It is chiefly written to make us excited about God's Word. It praises God's Word throughout and warns us against both the false teachers and against boredom and contempt for the Word. Therefore, it is primarily to be counted among the psalms of comfort.

– Martin Luther

GROUP BIBLE STUDY
(Questions and answers on pp. 170–71.)

1. Psalm 119 is an acrostic poem. Each eight-verse section of the lengthy psalm begins with the same letter of the Hebrew alphabet. English also uses acrostics. How many does your group know?

2. Hebrew poetry (the style of literature of the Psalms) is fond of parallelism (a statement or idea is reinforced by a second phrase that uses new imagery or vocabulary to say the same thing). What is the relationship between the two halves of verse 1?

3. What overall impression does this section of the psalm present? Do you think that the psalmist actually expects his readers to keep the Law? How does this fit with your understanding of the Law?

4. Often we are taught that the Law's real purpose is to show us our inability and our need for divine grace. How does the psalmist's persistent portrayal of the Law as a good and positive reality to be celebrated challenge this idea?

5. Consider verse 2. What do you think it means to seek God with all your heart? Why might it be argued that for fallen humans this is an impossible ideal?

OKAY TO COPY THIS PAGE.   62

6. How does a man seek and secure a sincere heart that is purely focused only on God and His plans?

7. In verse 5, the psalmist prays that his ways may be established. What does it mean to have one's ways established? What role does a man play in establishing his own ways?

8. Think about verse 6. Why would a man be ashamed when looking at (that is hearing and studying) God's commandments? How can this shame be a good thing?

9. What is something you have learned about God's Law for which you can give thanks today?

10. What would you tell someone who is feeling forsaken by God?

Blessed Is the Man © 2009 Concordia Publishing House. Reproduced by permission.

Week Three

Psalm 119:105–112

[105] Your word is a lamp to my feet
and a light to my path.

[106] I have sworn an oath and confirmed it,
to keep Your righteous rules.

[107] I am severely afflicted;
give me life, O Lord, according to Your word!

[108] Accept my freewill offerings of praise, O Lord,
and teach me Your rules.

[109] I hold my life in my hand continually,
but I do not forget Your law.

[110] The wicked have laid a snare for me,
but I do not stray from Your precepts.

[111] Your testimonies are my heritage forever,
for they are the joy of my heart.

[112] I incline my heart to perform Your statutes
forever, to the end.

Frank Fischer

Psalm 119:105

Your word is a lamp to my feet and a light to my path.

Light for Our Path

Have you ever had one of those "aha" moments? One when you later realized that at an important moment you'd failed to see something that was so obvious it should have blown you away? God's providential care for us can be like that. He directs our lives in so many ways every day, but we are often completely unaware of it. He moves and works throughout the circumstances of our lives. Sometimes we become more aware of this by the choices He presents or allows the evil one to present; other times it seems more direct.

In Jeremiah 29:11, the Bible tells us, "'For I know the plans I have for you,' declares the Lord, 'plans for welfare and not for evil, to give you a future and a hope.'"

I remember a time when we lived in Indianapolis. I had a great job with a good company. I was not looking for a job but was approached by two different companies in a short period of time to consider a new position that would not require relocating. Both jobs looked very attractive, and both offered a substantial financial increase, bonus potential, and career growth. As circumstance would have it, both jobs dried up (was it circumstance?). One company decided not to establish an operation in Indianapolis, and the other decided on an internal candidate. Two months later, my company announced its relocation to St. Louis.

I came down with a severe case of decision paralysis. We liked Indy. My family was relatively connected and involved with our church, and we liked the neighborhood we lived in. As time passed, I was strongly encouraged by management to move, given a salary increase, provided a signing bonus, and offered a full relocation package, yet I was still paralyzed. Finally, a call to our home directly from the CEO triggered our decision to move . . . again.

In retrospect, it is the best decision my family has ever made. We have lived in one home for the longest time in our family's history, over eleven years now. I have since departed that company and started one of my own. We are more grounded in our faith and involved with God's work than we ever thought would happen. We feel so at home with our friends and neighbors that its as if they were family members. Clearly, God had a plan to prosper us; we just weren't aware of the details. He opened and closed employment doors right before the move announcement just to let us know He was doing something. He even had a choir member at our church in Indianapolis tell us about this large church in St. Louis that had a big contemporary choir, where his sister sang, and that we should check it out. I shrugged it off and didn't even remember the name of the church or location when we moved . . . which is three miles away and the place we immediately joined that has forever changed our lives. Coincidence? Not a chance!

God is continuously involved in our day-to-day lives, whether we recognize it or not. His contact with us is not as dramatic as a cloud leading us, a voice from heaven, a burning bush, or even a hand appearing to write a warning. But that does not mean He is not intimately involved. We may not see Him working or recognize the signs, but the outcome is always in our best interest. God chose us and promises to take care of us. As Christian men, we need to learn to step back and be more objective about the circumstances of our lives. We are not in control as contemporary society leads us to believe. Once we realize that God is setting the stage of life, whether He's testing us or leading us, we will see more of the daily blessings He gives us, and the bad stuff will not seem to hurt as much.

God's Word is filled with direction for our lives. He gives us His commandments and expectations to communicate the parameters of a godly life. But then, knowing we cannot keep His commandments and meet His expectations, He sent His Son, Jesus. True, Jesus lived a perfect life as an example to us, "walking the walk and talking the talk," as it were. But He did even more than that. The point of His walking and talking was to save. God promises us eternal life with Him through faith in that same Jesus.

God's Word applied to the circumstances of our lives is a blessing. We may not be blessed by earthly standards, but we certainly are by God's standards. We have been given both Law and Gospel. The Law sets the expectations; it also serves as our compass. The Gospel shows us Jesus, our Savior; it also is the motor that drives our behavior in loving response to the forgiveness we receive by grace through faith.

In 1 Kings 2:3, we are told, "Keep the charge of the Lord your God, walking in His ways and keeping His statutes, His commandments, His rules, and His testimonies, as it is written in the Law of Moses, that you may prosper in all that you do and wherever you go." John 1:16–17 then states, "From His fullness we have all received grace upon grace. For the law was given through Moses; grace and truth came through Jesus Christ." It is clear that when God's Law and Gospel are applied to the direction and circumstances of our lives, blessings will ensue.

As we go through our earthly walk, we can choose from many intersecting paths. While some are clearly wrong paths, others are neither good nor bad, just different. While God knows what we will do, our choices are not predetermined. God's Word is the compass and motor with which we navigate life's paths. As Christian men, we listen to God speak to us through His Word and then applying God's Word to our circumstances. God chose us to be His sons and to be leaders in our families, churches, and communities. His Word is a lamp to our feet and a light to our path. Next time it's dark and you don't where to turn, let Him enlighten you. He'll show you the way.

....

While God knows what we will do, our choices are not predetermined. God's Word is the compass and motor with which we navigate life's paths.

Prayer: Dear God, too often I use my own reason and strength to brighten my way. Grant me Your grace, so that trusting in Christ alone, the light of the world, my life may be pleasing in Your sight. In Jesus' name. Amen.

....

Monday

DAILY STUDY QUESTIONS
Psalm 119:105

1. Think of a time when you were convinced that God was directing you through circumstances. How did you know it was God making it happen?

2. Are there any risks in reading circumstances to determine God's will?

3. Where does the psalmist look for direction when the way is unclear?

4. Is it circumstances alone, or are the paths that we travel inherently dark?

5. Since Christ is *the* Word, how does He illumine our paths?

Psalm 119:106–107

I have sworn an oath and confirmed it, to keep Your righteous rules. I am severely afflicted; give me life, O Lord, according to Your word!

Life by His Word

Are you the same man every day as you go through your routines? That might sound like a silly question at first, but in the context of today's verses, it may be something to ponder. The real question is this: Are you consistent? Do you think the same, behave the same, and talk the same at home, at work, in the gym, at your kids' sporting events, with close friends, or at church functions? Or are you a different man depending on the time, place, or people?

A popular television reality series, a game really, takes a diverse group of thirteen people and puts them in one house for ten weeks. During that time, contact with the outside world is not permitted—no TV, no radio, no newspapers, and no telephone, just each other. A goal of the game is to be one of two people left in the house after all the rest have been evicted. Another is to have made a positive connection with evictees, some of whom will ultimately comprise a jury. Each week, a grueling physical and/or mental competition determines the ruler for that week. This ruler nominates two individuals each week, one of which will be evicted by majority vote by the remaining players. Each week the number of players dwindles until there are only two remaining. The last six people evicted become the jury pool. That jury then decides which of the two players will be awarded $500,000.

The game is all about relationships and trust—or lack thereof. As power shifts, players are eliminated, and alliances are formed and broken, players demonstrate inconsistent behaviors. They lie, withhold information, get angry, feel betrayed, and lash out. Players, some of whom claim to be Christians, become manipulative and divisive in front of millions of viewers.

In many ways, this reality show is a condensed version of life. Most of us behave differently with different people in different places and under different circumstances. We manipulate a situation to our advantage. We spin the truth, exaggerate, or tell partial truths for "good" reasons. We get angry or even retaliate when we are hurt. We apply situational ethics to our decision making. We pursue agendas when cultivating relationships, such as trying to pacify the boss, hanging out with influential associates to get ahead, or spending time with attractive or fun people to make an impression. You get the point. But how does our daily behavior relate to our faith and our relationship with God?

At some point, most Christians have made an oath to Him. If you were baptized as a child, an oath was made on your behalf, but you affirmed that oath at your confirmation. If you came to faith when you were older, you may have made an oath at your Baptism. There are other oaths as well, such as marriage vows, promises we make to our kids, and contracts we sign with employers and customers. Whatever the event or timing, Christians make commitments, and with those commitments come responsibilities. The challenge is being consistent in living out our faith.

Can you think of a time that you have compromised an oath? I'm embarrassed to say that I can think of too many too easily. Some of the inconsistencies between what we promise and what we do are obvious, but more often than not, they are subtle. For example, telling "little white lies" and then trying to justify them in your mind. Or saying you have "another commitment" (when you don't), when you want to get out of a meeting (even at church) because you're too tired. Maybe you take unnecessary risks while driving because you procrastinated and are trying to make up the time. Maybe you don't help out around the house as much as you should or break your promises to your kids. There are thousands of ways for a man to be inconsistent and to break an oath.

I am not trying to make this sound worse than it is. But sin does sneak up on us. Sometimes breaking the oath is by commission, as described above. Sometimes it is by omission. But it is still wrong. Here's a tough one: How would you respond to a friend or co-worker when he or she tells an inappropriate joke? Would you laugh, respond with another, calmly correct the person, or walk away? God demands that we do what is right. Speaking with Cain, God said, "If you do well, will you not be accepted? And if you do not do well, sin is crouching at the door. Its desire is for you, but you must rule over it" (Genesis 4:7).

The oaths we make to God, our wives, our children, our employer, and our friends are important. When we're inconsistent from one day to the next, or try to be different men depending on the circumstances, people notice. God notices too. Looking at our failures, we will be humbled, or "severely afflicted" as the psalmist says (Psalm 119:106). But we are humbled also by God's grace. Our lives are not renewed by being perfect men but by being perfectly forgiven for the sake of Jesus.

Our life comes from His Word, which cleanses us. Jesus said, "Truly, truly I say to you, whoever hears My word and believes Him who sent Me has eternal life. He does not come into judgment, but has passed from death to life" (John 5:24). God Himself has sworn an oath that Jesus is our perfect forgiving priest, forever (Hebrews 7:15–28).

God's Word reminds us that He forgives us day in and day out. He blesses our lives and preserves us. Sometimes these blessings are in the midst of hardships, but all circumstances work to the good for us and according to His purpose. So the next time the Holy Spirit prompts you to do the right thing, keep your oath. Trust in Christ's mercy, and with the Lord's help seek to do what you have promised. God will never break His promises to You. His Word gives you light and life.

....

Our lives are not renewed by being perfect men but by being perfectly forgiven for the sake of Jesus. Our life comes from His Word, which cleanses us.

Prayer: Lord Jesus Christ, my great High Priest, forgive me for leading an inconsistent life. Help me to keep my word and not to break my promises. Help me to live a life pleasing to You so that others may hear Your Word and live. In Your name. Amen.

....

Tuesday

DAILY STUDY QUESTIONS
Psalm 119:106–107

1. In what ways is it true that every believer has sworn and made a commitment to live according to God's ways (commands)?

2. What part of your daily walk is presenting the greatest difficulty in the keeping of your promise to follow God's ways?

3. It has often been observed that the more serious one gets about living according to God's righteous ordinances, the more he seems to fail. Have you experienced this? Why might it be true?

4. What connection might there be between verses 106 and 107? How does affliction follow after a solemn promise?

5. Where does one look to find the reviving and life-sustaining Word of God?

Psalm 119:108-109

Accept my freewill offerings of praise, O Lord, and teach me
Your rules. I hold my life in my hand continually, but I do not
forget Your law.

God-Pleasing Speech

Did you hear about the guy tailgating the car in front of him because he was in a hurry? When the light turned amber, he planned to follow the car through an intersection. But to his surprise, the car stopped, so the guy had to slam his brakes to avoid a collision. The guy began screaming and cursing at the driver in front. A police officer, following in the rear, promptly arrested the guy in the middle car and took him to jail. A few hours later, the police officer released him from jail and apologized. The officer went on to explain, "When I saw how you were yelling, swearing, and using obscene hand gestures, all while driving a car with a WWJD sticker (What Would Jesus Do?), the fish symbol magnet, and a cross dangling from your rearview mirror, I assumed the car was stolen and took the appropriate action."

People watch what Christians say and do, good or bad. Yesterday, we talked about keeping our oaths and being consistent in all that we do. In today's verses, we consider our speech. God encourages us to speak in ways that are pleasing to Him. But this means more than just words. It also includes tone and intent of the heart. There is no place for gossip, condescension, or belittling speech that destroys people. Peter tells us, "Do not repay evil with evil or reviling with reviling, but on the contrary, bless, for to this you were called, that you may obtain a blessing. For, 'Whoever desires to love life and see good days, let him keep his tongue from evil and his lips from speaking deceit'" (1 Peter 3:9-10).

A few years back, my son, who was twenty-three years old at the time, had a drinking problem. It affected his well-being as well as his relationship with his mom and me. Since he still lived at home with us, I felt it was reasonable to expect that he would honor our rules. Most of our discussions, if you could call that that, started with me holding my ground, then resorting to shouting and threats that were neither healthy nor productive. At forty-eight, I still had some growing up to do. When I finally recognize that bullying him would never work, I tried a different approach:

patience and courtesy. When I stopped raising my voice and using inappropriate language to make a point or to get his attention, we started making progress. We still had to use "tough love," such as asking him to move out until he recognized he had a problem, but we were able to maintain a solid and supportive relationship. A year later, he moved back home. He has been dry for two years, is a good Christian man, and is one of my closest friends. I am ashamed to say that the Christian behavior I practiced in the professional business world I did not practice at home. I treated complete strangers better than my own son.

Clearly, displeasing speech is harmful and something to be avoided. But since speech is a gift from God, absence of pleasing speech is also a problem. I remember a rainy evening coming home from the airport after a business trip. It was 10:00 p.m. and I stopped for gas. The pay-at-the-pump did not work, so I went in to pay. I very intentionally carry a picture of Jesus in an obvious spot in my wallet, which is visible when I open it. The attendant commented, something like "nice picture," to which I responded, "Thanks," and went on my way. During the short drive home, I am sure I heard a rooster crow in my car. Perhaps the guy at the gas station was Christian and wanted to acknowledge our connection, or maybe he needed an ear, or perhaps he was not Christian and was curious. I will never know the impact of my failure to speak. I can only pray that God will use someone else to help that young man.

Even among my family and friends, I sometimes defer from speaking when I know I should. It is difficult to counsel people with whom I am close because I do not want to cause friction, sound pious, start an argument, or alienate them. Nevertheless, whether the subject is lack of church attendance, the use of foul language, gossiping about other people, or other questionable behavior, as a Christian father, husband, friend, and neighbor, I am obligated to lovingly and patiently step up.

Paul has a word to say about God-pleasing speech as well, "Therefore encourage one another and build one another up, just as you are doing" (1 Thessalonians 5:11.) While we should avoid destructive speech and not hold back when helpful criticism is appropriate, we should also not withhold encouraging and complimentary speech. People need encouragement, and those who offer it are often blessed as well. My best managers were people who noticed my work and took the time to compliment and encourage me. When they did, I was so motivated that I gave my best, which in turn helped them.

I try to encourage and compliment my wife regularly, being careful to avoid sounding redundant or patronizing. For example, when she has worked really hard on something, I thank her and tell her I appreciate what she does. Every so often, I tell her how important she is to me and for the well-being of our family. Compliments can be easy when you look for reasons to offer them and do not miss an opportunity to give them.

So don't be the guy in the car who screams and curses while a cross dangles from his rearview mirror. Through Jesus' death and resurrection, God has cleansed also your lips. Our Lord Jesus speaks a good word for us continually before our Father in heaven (1 John 2:1). Let that good word of your righteousness before God, received through the gift of faith, inspire you to praise Him before others.

> So don't be the guy in the car who screams and curses while a cross dangles from his rearview mirror. Through Jesus' death and resurrection, God has cleansed also your lips.

> *Prayer: Heavenly Father, forgive me for my unruly tongue and my sin-stained lips. Help me to use my words to encourage and uplift, not to tear down and destroy, so that others might praise Your name. I ask for the sake of Jesus, my Savior. Amen.*

Wednesday

DAILY STUDY QUESTIONS
Psalm 119:108–109

1. Think about the different ways you have used your mouth so far today. How much of it would you consider to be an offering to the Lord?

2. In verse 109, the psalmist indicates that he is continually in precarious situations—his life in his hands—yet he does not forget God's Law. How does a tough situation often lead to forgetting or at least minimizing God's Law?

3. What connection could be drawn between your use of words and finding yourself in a tight spot? Does your mouth ever get you into trouble?

4. How does remembering God's Law help us in our use of words and in our steadiness when we find ourselves in challenging circumstances?

5. What are some words of offering that need to come from your mouth today? Who needs to hear them?

Psalm 119:110–111

The wicked have laid a snare for me, but I do not stray from Your precepts. Your testimonies are my heritage forever, for they are the joy of my heart.

Leaving a Legacy

Earlier in my management career, I was hired as a new director. Two peers and I were charged with integrating a division of our company. Within three months and without my involvement, they were demoted and began reporting to me. Until that point, we had been getting along. But with the demotions, everything changed. One colleague resigned immediately. The other pretended everything was great, saying things like "no hard feelings" and that "we were fine" and so on. Nothing could have been further from the truth. My new report began bad-mouthing me to customers and employees and undermining me within the organization. Occasionally, I would hear secondhand about what was being said or done against me. In an attempt to repair the relationship, I worked diligently to support my colleague. I did not pursue any disciplinary action, which, in retrospect, was a big mistake. Obviously naïve, in this person's case I was a poor judge of character. It never occurred to me that someone would be intentionally divisive and destructive.

When we Christians live out our faith in the workplace, at home, or even on the ball field, we will fall victim to this sinful world. Jesus said, "I am sending you out as sheep in the midst of wolves, so be as wise as serpents and innocent as doves" (Matthew 10:16). He warns us that wicked people will harm us. We need to be alert and aware of traps and snares, while still being tolerant, forgiving, and resistant. While we are to turn the other cheek, we should not actively look for someone to strike us. Eventually, I addressed the issue with my new subordinate in a calm, professional manner. This person left the company shortly thereafter, and my reputation was restored, but not without a huge effort on my part to get things back on track. I could have been more assertive in dealing with my colleague's tactics. The trick for all of us is to find the right balance and acting as God intends.

Jesus was very familiar with the treachery of this world. Oh that we could have His insights! In Mark 12:13–17, the Pharisees attempted to trick Jesus by asking Him if they should pay taxes to Caesar. You probably know the story. Jesus said, "Give to Caesar what is Caesar's and to God what is God's" (Mark 2:17). We must comply with the rules of this world. We will also suffer the results of others' sin. But we cannot succumb to this world's temptations or be trapped by its snares.

The secular world, however, is not the only place where the devil does his work. At thirty, I was elected vice president of a congregation. During our first council meeting, the president resigned, leaving me with the reins. At the voter's meeting the following week, the ex-president moved to terminate the pastor for malfeasance. There was a significant division in the congregation. According to Scripture and confirmed by our denomination, I knew the pastor was innocent. Though he was unable to meet and in some cases even ignored the needs of a significant portion of the congregation, this was not due to his malfeasance. That the pastor also dug in his heels did not help. The whole situation deteriorated.

Both perspectives had merit, and some change in direction was needed to lead the flock. However, the approach to foster change was not constructive. Members did the wrong thing for what they genuinely believed to be the right reason. Instead of collaboration, there was persecution. Instead of tolerance, there were demands. Instead of negotiation, there were ultimatums. In Romans 12, and specifically verses 4–5, Paul describes the Church as being one Body made up of many parts. As Christian men, we work diligently at unity within the church. We actively forgive, explore alternative solutions to conflict, and mentor each other so our behavior is as Jesus taught and lived by example. That does not mean avoiding conflict. It means, rather, addressing conflict as Jesus articulates in Matthew 18:15–17. That could be a whole study by itself.

In Titus, Paul offers guiding principles for different groups in our society. He talks about how Christians are to behave for the sake of the Gospel. This book is kind of an instruction manual containing practical application of faith to the circumstances we experience in life. We are to teach others through example and outward encouragement. Our wives and children respond to our leadership—leadership that must be rooted in sound Christian behavior. It is impossible to tell your teenager to stop swearing and cursing if he or she hears you use foul language, to demand that your co-workers not lie if they observe you spinning the truth, and to expect that your wife remain calm and collected while you fly off the handle.

Our heritage and the joy of our heart are God's promises in His Word. Those promises, fulfilled in our Savior, Jesus Christ, create within us new hearts—hearts that trust God's testimonies and enliven us to good works. It is wonderful to see God's love in Christ reflected in the lives of other people. I am never so proud of my daughter as when she demonstrates her Christian character at work and in her marriage. I am never so proud of my son as when he demonstrates his Christian faith by coming to the aid of others and supporting friends. I am never so in love with my wife as when I see her compassion and commitment to the well-being of the family and others.

Whether you are married or not, young or older, no matter what your station in life, we Christian men reflect Christ in all we do. Our legacy is the example of our actions and positive influence as rooted in our faith and the good news of Jesus Christ. Yes, the wicked will lay snares for you. But God's Word of peace and reconciliation in Christ will bring you through.

Our heritage and the joy of our heart are God's promises in His Word. Those promises, fulfilled in our Savior, Jesus Christ, create within us new hearts.

Prayer: Dear Father, I have fallen into the devil's traps and have strayed from Your Word. Have mercy on me. Rescue me, renew my spirit, and lead me by Your grace, so that I may cling to Your promises. In Jesus' name. Amen.

Thursday

DAILY STUDY QUESTIONS
Psalm 119:110–111

1. Who are the "wicked" referred to in verse 110?

2. How might following God's ways make a man especially vulnerable to the snares of the wicked?

3. On the other hand, how does following God's ways guard us from falling prey to many wicked snares?

4. How are God's truth and His way of life comparable to an inheritance?

5. What kind of man would consider the laws and commands of God to be a source of great joy?

Psalm 119:112

I incline my heart to perform Your statutes forever,
to the end.

A Falling Star

It was a conflicted feeling—being in so much pain and yet filled with a strange, inner peace—all while strapped to a gurney. The panic in the paramedics' eyes and the urgency of their voices indicated they were not feeling the same sense of peace. But then, maybe they had not just spoken with their Lord. No, I had not heard an audible heavenly voice, had a vision, and seen anything so miraculous as a burning bush. But I did pray. I remember praying that God's will be done and thinking about what the apostle Paul said in Philippians 1:22–24, "If I am to live in the flesh, that means fruitful labor for me. Yet which I shall choose I cannot tell. I am hard pressed between the two. My desire is to depart and be with Christ, for that is far better. But to remain in the flesh is more necessary on your account."

December 1, 2007, was like any Saturday . . . at first. I was leading a great group of fellow volunteers to modify a stage platform and construct some props for the upcoming Christmas drama at church. After a morning of work and fellowship, our last task was to assemble and hoist a 20-foot star onto a 35-foot cross at the front of the sanctuary. The 225-pound three-dimensional star was made of metal conduit pipe attached to a center aluminum plate shrouded with a gold metallic cloth. We had used it before; it had been professionally engineered for its intended purpose. Only that day, some fatigued hardware snapped, and that star plummeted down and struck me in the back, then glanced off my hip before putting a 2-inch diameter hole through a ¾" plywood floor. We later found out that it broke my scapula (shoulder blade) in two places, three vertebrae, all the ribs on my left side multiple times, and punctured my left lung twice.

God answered my prayer that day right there in the ambulance. I sensed very strongly that I would recover. God had a plan and I was to be (a) patient—pun intended. Paul wrote to Timothy, "As for you, always be sober-minded, endure suffering, do the work of an evangelist, fulfill your ministry" (2 Timothy 4:5). Christians will not be free from pain or hardship in this sinful world. Jesus' followers will suffer much for the kingdom of God, so we must encourage each other (Acts 14:21–22). But that day, I felt that God was assuring me inwardly that things would be okay and to trust in Him. Psalm 112:4 says, "Light dawns in the darkness for the upright."

The next morning in the ICU, I began reflecting on what happened and why I might be the victim of such a freak accident. Shortly thereafter, a male nurse trying humor said to me that I must really be sideways with "the big Guy" if I got hurt doing His work in His house. Wow! I didn't see that coming. Knowing how our loving God protects and takes care of His own, it never even occurred to me that anyone could even think this would be a form of punishment. I missed the opportunity to talk with that young man about our loving God, but I would not miss another.

That's when it hit me. In my self-centered state, I thought this injury was all about me; how foolish! My accident was never about me, it was about God doing His work in all circumstances. He made sure I was fine and this was a mere setback. The psalmist says, "He is not afraid of bad news; his heart is firm, trusting in the LORD. His heart is steady, he will not be afraid" (Psalm 112:7–8).

Throughout my stay in the trauma ward, and even in the individual doctors' offices that I would visit for the next five months, I was affectionately known as "the star guy." The novelty of how and where the accident happened created opportunities to witness, probably much more than a typical injury. All this was by God's design. When they asked how the accident happened that December morning, I shared with them how blessed I was that God steered the star away from my head and all vital organs. I never needed surgery and would have no long-term debilities. This was truly a miracle.

God always seemed to prompt people to be curious, whether they were friends, neighbors, business associates, or strangers, they always asked. Sometimes God used my story in subtle ways, other times it was obvious the Holy Spirit was engaging them as current Christians or potentially interested parties. He worked through my injury and I was glad to serve His purposes. This perspective also helped my family and me to cope with the situation by turning our focus outward instead of inward.

A Christian man should never believe that God is retaliatory or vengeful. While He may allow things to happen to discipline us, it is always done with love and in our best interest. Sometimes, it's not even about us at all. In retrospect, I not only grew in my faith as a result of my accident, but my thirty-one-year marriage was made even stronger, and God impacted the people around me. God will recognize and reward the Christian man who has a steadfast heart, is secure in his faith, and trusts in Him. It may not be earthly honor or prosperity, but it will be everlasting.

Through His grace in Christ, God forgives us and makes us one of His own. Through the Gospel and Sacraments, He conforms us to the image of His Son. He inclines our hearts toward doing His will. God will never leave us or forsake us. Even when hardships enter our lives and doubts creep in, His Holy Spirit strengthens us and reminds us that we are His own. In Him, we will always triumph. No need to thank your lucky star; thank your heavenly Father.

....

Through the Gospel and Sacraments, [God] conforms us to the image of His Son. He inclines our hearts toward doing His will.

Prayer: Dear Lord, You protect me each and every day. Grant me a thankful heart, so that in all that You richly provide me, both body and soul, I might praise You both now and forever. Through Jesus Christ, Your Son. Amen.

....

Friday

DAILY STUDY QUESTIONS
Psalm 119:112

1. Why is choosing to live with a heart committed to God's ways no guarantee of a life free of suffering and difficulty?

2. When an evil event invades your life, what determines the sort of impact it will have on you and your character?

3. Reflecting back on your week, how might you have responded differently (with a heart more in focus on God's ways) to some of the surprise intrusions into your days?

4. Forever is a very long time! How is it possible for a human to promise to do anything forever?

5. Decide on one of God's statutes, and make a plan for how you are going to follow it today. (If you're drawing a blank, take a look at Exodus 20 or Matthew 5.)

Week Three

PSALM 119

[Psalm 119's] primary concern is that we have
God's Word in its purity and hear it gladly.
From this concern, then, come powerful prayers,
instructions, thanks, prophecies, worship of
God, suffering, and all that pleases God and
grieves the devil. But where one despises the
Word and is satiated by it, there all these cease.
For where the Word is not purely taught, there
is truly an abundance of prayers, instructions,
comforts, worship, suffering, and prophecies—
but totally false and condemned! For it is then
only service to the devil, who is thus impure
with all his heretics.

– Martin Luther

GROUP BIBLE STUDY
(Questions and answers are on pp. 175–77.)

1. Has your community ever passed a new law that made an impact on your day-to-day life? What did you think of the law?

2. Every one of the 176 verses of Psalm 119 contains some term referring to God's revealed will. Pick out each word in the verses studied this week. What different connotations does each word carry?

3. God's revealed will, the will of God for His creation, is more simply called the Law. How does a man learn this Law (see Romans 2:14–16; Deuteronomy 6:4–9)? Why do all men not universally recognize this Law?

4. What is the psalmist's attitude toward the Law? What is different about the way that a Christian understands the Law (see Galatians 3:19–26; Romans 7:12)?

5. Calling God's Word a lamp and a light (v. 105) is an apt metaphor that has long been a favorite of believers. How many different ways can your group think of to apply the metaphor? In other words, in what ways is God's Word a lamp and a light?

6. How does God's Word work to revive an afflicted soul? What role does weekly corporate worship (church!) and Bible study play in the revival of a soul?

7. What does James 3:7–12 teach us about the way we are to use our mouths? How might thinking about your words as a freewill offering to God (v. 108) help you to learn the lessons James wants us to learn?

8. How precarious is the life that you live? What sorts of snares are set in your path? Who puts them there? What kind of harm will they inflict? How dangerous are they?

9. In what sense is your Church (in all of its senses: congregation, denomination, and church invisible—militant and triumphant) an inheritance that has been granted to you? What responsibility do you have to pass this inheritance to others? Are you leaving your children an inheritance equal to the one you received?

10. What things will you do this coming week to more fully incline your heart to know, do, and delight in God's Law?

Week Four

Psalm 127

[1] Unless the LORD builds the house,
those who build it labor in vain.
Unless the LORD watches over the city,
the watchman stays awake in vain.

[2] It is in vain that you rise up early
and go late to rest,
eating the bread of anxious toil;
for He gives to His beloved sleep.

[3] Behold, children are a heritage from the LORD,
the fruit of the womb a reward.

[4] Like arrows in the hand of a warrior
are the children of one's youth.

[5] Blessed is the man
who fills his quiver with them!
He shall not be put to shame
when he speaks with his enemies in the gate.

Bob Morris

Psalm 127:1

Unless the LORD builds the house, those who build it labor in vain. Unless the LORD watches over the city, the watchman stays awake in vain.

Off We Go

I love airplanes; always have. My childhood home was near a small U.S. Army airfield. The mechanics and pilots there wondered who was that ten-year-old sitting for hours outside the "Do Not Enter" sign near the hanger just to catch a glimpse of them as they serviced or piloted the airplanes. One day an Army pilot walked out to me as I sat by the sign. He took me to an airplane in the hanger where he showed me the cockpit with its array of instruments. It would be many years before I would sit before such instruments as a private pilot.

Although I had a successful twenty-six-year career in the U.S. Air Force and had spent many hours in airplanes as a passenger, my eyesight prevented my becoming an Air Force aviator. Still, the urge to become a pilot never left. So, at fifty-eight, I went to aviation ground school at a local college, completed the course, passed the FAA written exam, and began flight training for a private pilot's license. Psalm 127:1 makes a great template for a student pilot because of its emphasis on reverence, commandments, and rewards as the Lord "builds our house."

My greatest fear as I began training was not crashing but getting lost. From above, practically nothing on the ground can look familiar. Just flying the airplane, observing the instruments, working the radio, watching out for other airplanes, and seeing the ground move beneath at a high speed were challenging enough. Keeping track of my location at the same time seemed insurmountable at first. As the training progressed, however, I gained great respect for the aviation maps and the various navigational aids, and my fear subsided.

Of course, the deep reverence for God implied in Psalm 127:1 infinitely surpasses the respect a pilot has for navigational aids, but there is a parallel. A pilot learns to navigate wisely by respecting the tools provided, such as maps, global positioning systems, and other means. A Christian begins to learn how to navigate the pathways of life with wisdom by commencing with a deep reverence for the Lord (Psalm 111:10). Scripture reading, reception of the Sacrament, and godly counsel help ensure that whatever we do, whether building a house, watching over a city, or piloting a plane, is not done in vain.

Pilot training also entails learning and applying many rules and regulations and following the directions of flight instructors. One obvious flight rule is to avoid obstacles such as TV and radio towers and their support cables. I had just taken off at an airport and was at a sufficient altitude when the flight instructor turned off the radio and all navigation aids except for the magnetic compass. He then told me to fly us back to the home airport using the compass, which I proceeded to do with what I proudly thought was skill for a beginning student pilot. Just a few minutes into the flight, he turned to me and asked, "Do you see a problem?" I looked at my heading and around me and saw no problem. About a minute later, he asked the same question. Again, I saw no problem. He then informed me that we had a TV tower 1,977 feet in height straight ahead. "Turn west now," he instructed. I did. When flying to this airport from which I had just departed, the instructor had given specific instructions about the tower. Before we had departed the home airport, he had pointed out the tower on the aviation map. He had essentially given a command to avoid it. In my zeal to prove my ability to get us home, I had neglected to remember the command. I had disobeyed. The lesson learned that day was stamped into my permanent memory bank.

Such is life when we neglect to delight in God's commandments and disobey Him. This is sin. When I did not follow my instructor's command, it could have had dire consequences. Sin also has consequences. Thankfully, we have forgiveness for our sins through the blood of our Savior, the Lord Jesus Christ. I believe we can delight in His commandments not only because they are supremely perfect—although we cannot be perfect following them—but also because Jesus perfectly followed them for us. We can delight that we can be forgiven by Him when we disobey His commands and delight that His forgiveness has eternal implications.

Just as there are consequences for disobedience, there are also rewards for obedience. After a student pilot has successfully completed all the rigorous training requirements and has passed the FAA tests and flight evaluation, he or she is finally issued the pilot's license. The student pilot has been rewarded based on flying ability and for demonstrating a knowledge of and respect for the many aviation rules, regulations, and directives. From the spiritual perspective, those who deeply reverence God, delight in His commandments, and seek by God's grace to obey them will be rewarded also. God does not reward our actions with salvation, but there are rewards in this life and the next. The Lord promises to remember the righteous ones forever (Psalm 112:6).

In Psalm 127:1, we see how all human toil without God is in vain. Without God, our plans are meaningless. But with God, life is full of meaning and purpose. We see that especially in the cross. There, where God reconciled us through the broken body and poured-out blood of Jesus, He declares us righteous, and our eternity is secured. When God remembers a righteous man forever, that means God's everlasting love, care, and comfort go with that man. In whatever we do, building houses, watching cities, or even in flying aircraft, we know we have a competent Pilot who will make sure we arrive safely home.

....

In Psalm 127:1, we see how all human toil without God is in vain. Without God, our plans are meaningless. But with God, life is full of meaning and purpose.

Prayer: Dear God, be part of my life every day. Forgive me for taking pride in my strength and accomplishments, and help me to rely more and more upon Your grace. I ask this through Jesus, Your Son, our Lord. Amen.

....

Monday

DAILY STUDY QUESTIONS
Psalm 127:1

1. If the Lord builds the house, what part do you need to play? How does a Christian man build and watch when God is the one who is to build and watch?

2. What does it look like when a man is laboring in vain? What are some examples of futile work?

3. Why are building and watching good metaphors for the responsibility of a Christian man?

4. Have you ever found yourself on a collision course with a "TV broadcast antenna"? What deadly threats have suddenly appeared in the "good course" you have charted?

Psalm 127:2

It is in vain that you rise up early and go late to rest, eating the bread of anxious toil; for He gives to His beloved sleep.

Be at Peace

"The tumor on your pancreas is inoperable and may become malignant."

The appointment with my father's long-time physician was surprisingly short and to the point. When it was over, my father, mother, and I returned to their car numbed by the experience. Earlier, I had sensed something was not routine when the physician requested that Mother and I accompany Dad to his appointment. This began a six-month journey of learning through experience the lessons of Psalm 127:2. Ultimately, this verse reminds us Christians to have faith in God, not to be anxious, and that He will give us peace in all circumstances.

Because Dad's other medical conditions would have most likely precluded a successful outcome, his physician stated that Dad's condition was inoperable. However, Dad had always been one to take risks, so he elected to have part of his pancreas removed by one of Atlanta's top surgeons. The surgical procedure went well, but, as my dad's primary physician had suspected, there were complications. In time, there was the ventilator, then loss of hearing and speaking, then paralysis, then infections, then one life-threatening condition after another. Dad was slowly losing the battle as one by one the bodily systems so essential to life began to fail. Early one morning, after five months of acute and intensive care, my Christian father departed this mortal life to be with the Lord.

This was not a pleasant journey the family had taken with Dad, but the precepts in Psalm 127:2 lightened the load. To be honest, the stress of the setbacks, the suffering, the long hospital stays, and everything else associated with a critical illness did provide a medium for anxiety, but faith in God's all-knowing and loving care ultimately prevailed over fear, and a certain peace was present throughout those months.

In Matthew 6:25–34, Jesus addresses anxiety. He reveals how well He knows us. Among a multitude of concerns, we can be anxious about the very basics of life, such as food, clothing, drink, work, and anything to do with our mortal bodies. Jesus specifically mentions those areas in this passage. He commands us not to worry about our lives. He reminds us that our heavenly Father, who provides for animals and plants, will certainly take care of us, whom He loves more than we can comprehend.

In verse 34, Jesus commands us to take one day at a time and not to worry about what tomorrow will bring. During my father's medical journey, I tried to take one day at a time; sometimes one hour at a time. The events of some days were so challenging that I needed to live only that day and not think about the next. Other trying events during my life have been similar to that. It is not always easy to not worry and to just let the concerns of the day suffice, as Jesus directs.

Reaching the point where we do not worry about life's issues requires a deep faith that God knows what is best and that He will take care of us. Only God can give us that kind of faith, which Jesus says comes by seeking God's kingdom and His righteousness first (Matthew 6:33). As we repent of trusting in ourselves even for basic necessities, through the Gospel of His Son, God enables us to believe that He will care for us. His Holy Spirit, the Divine Comforter, works and strengthens such faith through the reading, hearing, and studying of God's Word. Such faith is exercised through prayer.

God tells us to "pray without ceasing" (1 Thessalonians 5:17). This means we are to use prayer daily as we go about our activities. I certainly prayed often during my father's illness. Sometimes a prayer can be as short as "help." Other prayers can be words of rejoicing (v. 16) or giving thanks (v. 18). The model prayer for us is given by our Lord Jesus in Luke 11:2–4. God hears the prayers of the righteous (Proverbs 15:29). The Holy Spirit Himself intercedes for us when we do not know for what we should be praying (Romans 8:26). As we pray God's promises back to Him, God strengthens our faith.

We are blessed to have God's Word. We are to meditate on it (Joshua 1:8); those are blessed who hear and obey it (Luke 11:28); it was written to bring us to faith in Jesus (John 20:31); it (the Gospel) is the power of salvation (Romans 1:16); it works faith (Romans 10:17); it destroys but also makes alive (2 Corinthians 3:6); and Christ builds His Church with it (Ephesians 2:20). God's Word is a sure antidote for anxiety.

We are also blessed to have the Holy Spirit. The Holy Spirit regenerates (John 3:5); indwells (Romans 8:11); anoints (1 John 2:20, 27); baptizes (Acts 2:17–41); guides (John 16:13); enables (Micah 3:8); sanctifies (Romans 15:16); bears witness (Romans 8:16); helps (John 14:16–26); gives joy (Romans 14:17); gives discernment (1 John 4:1–6); causes to bear fruit (Galatians 5:22–23); comforts (Acts 9:31); and reveals the things of God (1 Corinthians 2:10,13). What a faith-builder the Holy Spirit is!

The last sentence in Psalm 127:2 says the result of such faith and trust in God is "rest." What comes to my mind when rest is mentioned are those occasional ten-minute daytime naps that are so refreshing. What also comes to mind is a calm good night's sleep undisturbed by worry.

I want such peace when the trials of life buffet me. Through His Word and Spirit, our Lord Jesus grants us such serenity. He enables us to devote our lives to Him. He gives us a sincere faith and trust that He will take care of us now, at the end of our lives, and after we're gone. Even when the diagnosis of this life is grim, the diagnosis of our Great Physician, who suffered, died, and rose again for us, is always great.

....

I want such peace when the trials of life buffet me. Through His Word and Spirit, our Lord Jesus grants us such serenity.

Prayer: Dear God, in the midst of all the trials of life, be my guide. Grant me strength and courage to face the challenges of each day, knowing that through Christ, Your dear Son, I have Your peace. In Jesus' name. Amen.

....

Tuesday

DAILY STUDY QUESTIONS
Psalm 127:2

1. What is it that makes your labor today painful?

2. In what ways is walking through a long illness (yourself or with a loved one) a form of hard labor?

3. Psalm 127:2 almost seems to be the despairing cry of a cynic or skeptic. In what ways is it true that long hard labor is vain?

4. Interestingly, the psalmist turns the observation of man's futile labor to a word of comfort—although man can't *find* comfort, God can give it—even when man does nothing (i.e., is asleep). What is the relationship between human labor and divine provision?

5. The Hebrew of this verse is not readily translated (hence many variations among the English translations), but it is clear that sleep or rest is good and a gift from God. Is rest a means toward more energy for work, or is it the goal?

Psalm 127:3

Behold, children are a heritage from the LORD, the fruit of
the womb a reward.

A Heritage and a Reward

While we were having lunch together on a towboat heading down the Mississippi River, a towboat captain told me an amazing story. He was a seasoned mariner whose first career was with the United States Army. The Army has oceangoing ships that transport logistical supplies, equipment, vehicles, and weapons such as tanks and cannons. He became a captain of such a ship while an Army officer and was now enjoying his second career as a towboat captain after retiring from the Army.

He was born and raised in Borneo. This island, the third largest in the world, is located in maritime Southeast Asia, with the South China Sea to the north and northwest and the Philippines to the northeast. Indonesia, Malaysia, and Brunei govern the three regions of the island. The captain was from the region governed by Indonesia. The story of how he went from Borneo to becoming a United States Army officer will not be related here. What will be told occurred when he was in the Atlantic Ocean transporting cargo to Kuwait.

While sailing east in the Atlantic, an oil tanker flying the Indonesian flag was sailing west nearby. As a matter of courtesy, the ship captains greeted one another on the maritime radio frequency. Noting the origin of the tanker, the Army ship captain began to converse in the language of Borneo. Since his language was coming from a United States Army vessel, the tanker's captain was amazed and asked how the other captain became so fluent. He explained that he was born and raised in Borneo. Astounded, the tanker captain asked which town the Army ship's captain was from. He told him and, with surprise, the tanker captain said that was his hometown too. The oiler captain then asked where the other captain lived in the town. He identified the street and specific location. There must have been a long pause before the tanker captain replied, "My name is _____, and I am the boy who lived behind you who was nine years younger than you." They proceeded to recall childhood memories and bring each other up to date with what each knew about their old neighborhood and what happened to childhood friends. Two boys raised in the same neighborhood, from a far off island in the South China Sea, both becoming sea captains and meeting one another heading in opposite directions in the vast Atlantic Ocean—this is a remarkable story about what many would call pure coincidence.

While children are "a heritage from the LORD" (Psalm 127:3), raising them is no easy task. Countless books have been written about child rearing. While it is a complex subject, just three aspects having biblical foundations will be covered here. These are love, obedience, and wisdom. Unfortunately, Christian parents or a single parent or guardian(s) can raise a child properly and have the child go the way of the world later. These children may be a "reward" at birth, but that may not be the case later because of the grief or hardship they cause. Ceaseless and fervent prayer for these lost loved ones must be made for as long as possible.

All children need love, and 1 Corinthians 13:4–8 gives the attributes of love: it is patient, it is kind, it is not envious, it is not boastful, and it is not arrogant or rude. The love referred to in these verses is a Christlike love, better described in the Greek as agape love. Interestingly, the attributes are action words, something someone does to show love. The action implied with each word is applicable to everyone who is responsible for a child's care and development. Is it possible to perfectly adhere to these attributes of love at all times? No, we are imperfect and sinful in nature. Thankfully, God is merciful, and He forgives our sins, including the sin of lovelessness.

Children also need to be taught obedience to God and others in authority over them. Love is the fulfilling of the Law. Jesus says in Matthew 22:37 that the greatest and first commandment is to love the Lord our God with all our hearts, souls, and minds. Deuteronomy 6 instructs us to teach our children God's commandments and have them think on them often so that they will be in their hearts. In addition, we are to teach children to revere God (v. 24), to serve Him (v. 13), and to do what is good and right in His sight (v. 18). Children are not only a heritage for a family, they are also a heritage for a nation as well. Deuteronomy 28 gives the consequences of obedience and disobedience as they impact a man and a nation, and the Bible is replete with specific examples of blessings and judgment for both.

Wisdom, like obedience, is also dependent upon a deep reverence for God. Wisdom must be imparted to children by training (Proverbs 22:6) and by setting an example. Wisdom here is not worldly wisdom but rather wisdom from above. Worldly wisdom arises from the unrestrained and disbelieving heart. For from this heart, Jesus said in Matthew 15:19, proceeds all sorts of evil. In contrast, wisdom from above is "first pure, then peaceable, gentle, open to reason, full of mercy and good fruits, impartial and sincere" (James 3:17). The fear (faith-filled awe and reverence) of the Lord is wisdom's beginning (Psalm 111:10). The first step in wisdom is repentant faith in Jesus Christ. With wisdom from above, we discern and conduct our lives in a spiritual dimension and not a worldly one. Spiritual wisdom is living according to the love of God in Christ Jesus, our Savior. Those who have such wisdom are rewards and are a heritage to our faith.

Many would say the two sea captains originally from Borneo met each other in the Atlantic Ocean only by coincidence. Do you really think so? Children do not become responsible and successful adults by chance. Love, obedience, and wisdom are necessary. May God through His rich mercy in Christ Jesus give us the godly love, obedience, and wisdom we need in order to impart faith and godly living to the next generation.

....

Spiritual wisdom is living according to the love of God in Christ Jesus, our Savior. Those who have such wisdom are rewards and are a heritage to our faith.

Prayer: Dear Father in heaven, You made me Your child in Holy Baptism. Through Your Word and Sacraments, strengthen my faith so that I may be a good influence for those who follow after me. I ask this through Christ, our Lord. Amen.

....

Wednesday

DAILY STUDY QUESTIONS
Psalm 127:3

1. Would your parents say that *you* have been a gift and a reward?

2. How is it true that even a "disappointing" child is still a gift and a reward?

3. How does our society think about children? Does our culture, act as if they are a gift and reward from God? Do we?

4. How does recognizing children as God's gift make a difference in how we raise them?

5. How important is a child's upbringing en route to the goal of that child truly being a gift to others?

Like arrows in the hand of a warrior are the children of one's youth.

No Need to Drift

Chesapeake Bay was just about a hundred yards from my boyhood home in Virginia. It was a wonderful place to grow up watching the oceangoing ships coming into port and sailing out to sea, having a lighthouse nearby, seeing the fishing boats, and finding all kinds of interesting things that washed up on the beach. This ocean debris drifted with the tides and the changing currents with no definite direction or destination. Now my home is near the Mississippi River, where the debris moves differently. It is determined to head steadfastly in one direction: downstream. The destination may be New Orleans or the Gulf of Mexico, or it may go ashore elsewhere. Still, it seems to have a purpose.

Young people can resemble items floating on the water. Some just drift along, going in no particular direction. Others head in a set direction with a purpose. There are times in our lives when we men can influence those young people. They do not have to be our own children. These days, there are many young people who need caring, Christian male mentors to assist them. Johnny, Ron, and Seth were three such young people.

Johnny was a fifteen-year-old. He was making average to below average grades because he did not apply himself academically. He was more interested in play and getting into mischief at school than in studying. Although he was a Christian, Johnny didn't attend church regularly. He liked people and had the potential to do well in life but showed little interest or motivation to use his talents. I liked Johnny and arranged for him and his pastor to take an orientation flight in a small airplane with a flight instructor. The young flight instructor greeted Johnny with an enthusiastic smile. He gave Johnny a thorough orientation on the ground. In the air, he let Johnny fly for a while. After the flight, the instructor complimented Johnny on how well he did. At the time, I did not perceive that Johnny had much interest in aviation, but I later learned that the seed had been planted.

I lost track of Johnny, but about ten years later someone gave me an update on his life. He was now an aircraft maintenance specialist in the U.S. Air Force stationed in Japan with his wife and two children. Off-duty, he studied for his college degree, and he was doing well with his career. Once he told his parents that the orientation flight changed his life and that it had led him to enlist in the Air Force after high school graduation. God used just one half hour of flight time to change Johnny's life.

Ron was seventeen, a senior in high school, and a Christian active in his church. He did well academically, was never in trouble, and was sociable. Ron was being raised by his mother, who loved him very much. He just did not know what to do after he graduated. Either he had not thought much about college or was intimidated by the prospect. I took Ron to a local community college where he could talk to admissions, academic, and financial-aid counselors. He carried a basketball to our appointments and during the campus orientation. When I later asked him why, he said, "So people will think I am somebody," meaning people would think he was one of the school athletes. I do not remember what I said in response, but I always encouraged him and tried to make him feel special, which he was.

Weeks later, I also took him to a local, four-year major university because he was capable of the work. Again, like a parent I assisted him with all the procedures for admittance, including financial aid. Ron was accepted with financial assistance and went on to complete several years of university work. The last I heard of Ron several years ago, he was working with a car dealership, but I also suspect he may have gone back by now to complete his degree. Ron was certainly a valuable arrow in the hand of his mother.

Seth was thirteen and was a Christian from a single-parent family. He did not attend church regularly. His mother, also a Christian, had to work most Sundays. Seth was one of the most honest, thoughtful young men I had ever met. He had integrity and much maturity for someone his age. He was very intelligent and observant and wanted to become an engineer. Big for his age, he played football. He had just begun eighth grade, and his mother was worried about Fs on his report card. One Saturday, I asked him what he thought the problem was, and he told me. He rode the school bus each morning without having eaten breakfast, because the trip to school made him sick to his stomach. He ate a sweet at school for breakfast, and that is how the day began.

Another problem was homework. His mom insisted that he spend hours on homework, but after spending too much time on a particular subject, it became confusing to him. With his permission, I later passed these feelings and others on to his mom. I also recommended they begin to read the Bible and pray daily together. She was a good friend of mine and appreciated the input. Seth began to receive a healthy breakfast at home, his mom started driving him to school when possible, and she let Seth become responsible for doing his homework. Bible readings and prayer time hopefully began. Thankfully, his grades improved, and Seth had a successful school year. Seth is already an arrow and a blessing to both his mother and to me.

The blessings of influencing children at a young age will become evident as they grow older. I know of Christian men of all ages who have served as mentors to young people. They became those arrows to their families and to others spoken of in Psalm 127:4. By the power of the Holy Spirit, God can use us men to point young people to that anchor of hope we have in our Savior, Jesus Christ (Hebrews 6:19). There's no need for them to drift along aimlessly in their lives. In Christ, their lives, and ours, have purpose.

....

By the power of the Holy Spirit, God can use us men to point young people to that anchor of hope we have in our Savior, Jesus Christ (Hebrews 6:19).

Prayer: Lord God, thank You for all of the positive role models You provided for me when I was young. By Your grace, help me to recognize the opportunities where I can provide guidance to those who need it. I ask this for Jesus' sake. Amen.

....

Thursday

DAILY STUDY QUESTIONS
Psalm 127:4

1. Why would Solomon, today's psalmist, compare a man's children to a warrior's arrows?

2. Does our culture today value children the same way that the Israelites did? What evidence is there to support your answer?

3. The devotion offered three examples of young men receiving loving direction. While children are arrows that have minds of their own, how important is it for a father to aim and guide each arrow in his hand?

4. What happens when an arrow is poorly aimed? Who is responsible? How does this put a sharp point to the significance of a father's role?

Psalm 127:5

Blessed is the man who fills his quiver with them!
He shall not be put to shame when he speaks with his enemies
in the gate.

A Sterling Reputation

In 1967, as a very young man, I had the privilege of crossing the Atlantic Ocean on the SS United States sailing from Le Havre, France, to New York City. She is the fastest ocean liner ever built and still holds the record time for crossing the Atlantic Ocean for ships in her class. An incident occurred on this voyage that can be related to Psalm 127:5.

We had been at sea for several days when this 990-foot, swiftly moving ship came to a dead stop in the North Atlantic. A crew member onboard had died. The next of kin back home was notified and, apparently with the crew member's prior wishes, asked that he be buried at sea. The ship's captain honored the request. This great ship was stopped, and the body of the deceased crewman was lowered, and then committed to the depths of the ocean. The ship was far out at sea, at least ten thousand feet of water were underneath, and the family of the deceased was in some distant land. This incident is a reminder of just how small we are in this universe (Psalm 8:3–4) and of how transient are our lives on earth (James 4:14).

Our passing from this life to the next leaves to those who remain the memories of us and of our reputation. This crew member apparently had a sterling reputation since the SS United States was brought to a full stop for him. Stopping a ship meant time taken from a lengthy journey, and time is money for a commercial operation. He must have worked many dedicated years as a seaman and done his job well. A good reputation is apparently what he left with his shipmates, family, friends, and acquaintances. "He shall not be put to shame when he speaks with his enemies at the gate" in Psalm 127:5 is about a man's reputation, his good name. Reputation is built around a man's character. The trials of life, being a servant, and obedience build Christian character.

Some of the people that I admire and respect greatly are waiters or waitresses.

I prefer to call them servers, and I am refering to those who are truly adept in their trade. They project an attitude of "I am here to take care of you to the best of my ability." They have a certain humility and attitude that are refreshing, and at the same time, they maintain an admirable professionalism. Caregivers, such as nurses, can impress me that way too. Leaders, if they properly respond to the role, are servants. I have worked for superiors who behaved as servants; they cared about, mentored, informed, and supported the workforce. They set the example of integrity, the work ethic, and high standards. The workers did their best because they did not want to let this type of leader down. In Matthew 20:26, Jesus defined the Christian's role in life as one of being a servant. Even our Savior, Creator of the universe, says that He came to serve and not to be served (v. 28). When we consider ourselves as humble servants, it completely changes our outlook on life. Taking on the role of a servant in all that we do and say dramatically affects our character and how people will view our reputation while we live and after we are gone from this world.

Teaching obedience is a key influence on character development, and being obedient is a character trait. Obedience to God and listening to His voice are stressed throughout the Bible and Psalm 127. As parents or guardians, we are to teach children to fear God and follow His commandments. We are to instill within them the need for a lifetime of prayer, Bible study, and worshiping with fellow believers. These actions are vital foundations for Christian character building. Just one of many examples given in the Bible of disobedience and its consequences is in 1 Samuel 15. King Saul disobeyed God when he did not destroy all the Amalekites and all their possessions as God commanded. Instead, Saul spared their king, Agag, and the best of their possessions, including sheep, oxen, and lambs. Because of Saul's actions, God rejected Saul's kingship, ceased empowering him, and allowed psychological problems to torment him from then on. Saul's character was now flawed and his reputation soiled. He was "put to shame" (Psalm 127:5). Repenting of our sins, by the saving grace of our Lord Jesus Christ, we are forgiven for our disobedient and rebellious ways.

Let us again go out to the North Atlantic on the SS United States. We can deeply reflect on life and death there. In life did we grow closer to God through His Means of Grace, or did we depart from Him? Did we serve God and man, or did we insist on being served? Did we strive during our life to be obedient to God and to legitimate authority, or were we rebellious and unrepentant? A burial at sea is a stark reminder of death and of the time we will stand before the Lord Jesus to give an account of our lives.

A quiver full of children is a great blessing, because many children can bear witness to your reputation, especially before those who oppose you. But others bear witness too. Through faith in Christ, our reputation before the God who both made the seas and stilled them by His Word is perfect. Because of Christ's death and His victory over death, we need not fear either grave or sea. His Spirit, who hovered over the waters at creation and over the baptismal waters of our re-creation, inspires confidence and hope. Let us strive to be men of Christian character with sterling reputations both now and after we have departed this life. May Jesus say to us one day, "Well done, good and faithful servant. . . . Enter into the joy of your master" (Matthew 25:23).

....

Through faith in Christ, our reputation before the God who both made the seas and stilled them by His Word is perfect.

Prayer: Gracious God, forgive me for those times I have failed to live up to my status as Your son. Help me to live my life worthy of Your calling, so that my family, friends, and co-workers see my life as a reason to speak well of You. I ask this for Jesus' sake. Amen.

....

Friday

DAILY STUDY QUESTIONS
Psalm 127:5

1. Blessed is the man with a quiver full of children! Clearly, the psalmist sees a large family with many children as a gift from God. Is this simply a reflection of his rural society, or is there a blessing in having many children?

2. The psalm operates with a definite sense of what is important in life. What important things are highlighted in verse 5?

3. What is the relationship between a man's children and that man's reputation?

4. What sort of enemies would a man meet in the city gate (the ancient halls of business and social converse)? What enemies will face you today? How has God equipped you to handle them?

Week Four

PSALM 127

The 127th psalm is a psalm of instruction. It teaches us that worldly authority and house- hold order are nothing less than God's gifts and rest only in His hand. For where He does not give peace and good government, there no wisdom, order, exertion, or armor can hold onto peace. Where He does not give good fortune, with wife, children, and workers, there all care and work will be for nothing.

                                    – Martin Luther

GROUP BIBLE STUDY
(Questions and answers are on pp. 180–82.)

1. What was the worst job you ever had? What was it about the job that made it the worst?

2. Psalm 127 breaks into two distinct parts. How would you describe the topic of each, and what is the relationship between them?

3. Is Solomon being cynical (a charge often leveled at Ecclesiastes as well) in the first two verses of this psalm, suggesting that since there is no point to working hard (God is the one in charge anyway), why bother? If not cynicism, what is the motivation and message of these verses?

4. What is the right understanding of the relationship between human effort and divine activity? In other words, how can I be working hard at something when the success or failure of what I am doing depends entirely on God's intervention and activity?

5. How are building and watching particularly apt descriptions of the work of a Christian man? What sorts of building projects occupy his attention? In what areas must a Christian man be an adept watchman?

6. Why is it a matter of obedience and good stewardship to assure that times of hard labor are balanced with times of rest and sleep? Why have Christians sometimes had a hard time learning this? Do you think this is still an issue with people today?

7. Why would the psalmist so highly exalt the blessing of children? What are some of the blessings that come with having children?

8. Maternal instincts are well-known, and we have all seen the way that babies have a magnetic affect on women. What special roles do fathers have in the life of their children?

9. Christians are often eager to find Christ in every verse of the Bible—sometimes in spite of what the words might actually say. Think again about this psalm and consider where one may recognize the presence of Christ, or truths that point to His truth.

10. What concrete, tangible changes does this psalm call you to make this week?

Week Five

Psalm 128

[1] Blessed is everyone who fears the LORD,
who walks in His ways!

[2] You shall eat the fruit of the labor of your hands;
you shall be blessed, and it shall be well with you.

[3] Your wife will be like a fruitful vine
within your house;
your children will be like olive shoots
around your table.

[4] Behold, thus shall the man be blessed
who fears the LORD.

[5] The LORD bless you from Zion!
May you see the prosperity of Jerusalem
all the days of your life!

[6] May you see your children's children!
Peace be upon Israel!

Steve Sandfort

Psalm 128:1

Blessed is everyone who fears the Lord, who walks in His ways!

The Trail Boss

During my college days, I spent a couple summers working as a horse wrangler on a Colorado ranch. Each morning, against the backdrop of the majestic Rockies, I could be found leading a group of horses and riders down a well-worn trail through a forest of ponderosa pines. One lesson I learned during those days was that horses could be great followers. I'll never forget looking back at a long line of seven-foot tall, thirteen-hundred-pound animals following head to tail behind me. Sometimes I wish I could follow God as surely and trustingly as those horses followed my horse.

As the trail boss, it was my job to see that the path was clear and safe for our horses and guests. I also set the pace. If we rode too quickly, certain horses would pull out of line and make a run for the stables, depositing their screaming cargo along the way. If we rode too slowly, the line would begin to fold up on itself like an accordion, inevitably leading the cantankerous ones to kick and bite—the horses, that is. If everything went according to plan, the ride was blessed with peaceful mountain views and only the sounds of the wind through the trees and the clip clop of hooves on the trail.

In some respects, God is our trail boss for life's path. Walking in His ways and following His commands is how we find safety on the trail. Following this trail boss brings us the blessing of a beautiful journey filled with the peace that passes all understanding.

The psalmist writes, "Blessed is everyone who fears the LORD, who walks in His ways!" As an emotion, fear certainly places most men in a quandary. What father hasn't been "set up" by his own children with the words, "My dad's not afraid of anything"? But the fear of the Lord does not mean that I am afraid of God. Rather, it means that I am in awe of what God is capable of doing and being in my life. The fear of God is "hatred of evil" (Proverbs 8:13) and "the beginning of knowledge"

(Proverbs 1:7); it is the awe and reverence for Him in our hearts because He has given us forgiveness of sins, life, and salvation. We fear the Lord and walk in His ways because He is the trail boss, leading us down the path and through the narrow gate to everlasting life.

God is a trustworthy trail boss. However, we are not always faithful riders. The devil and our sinful nature lead us away from the narrow path and into the wild grasses this world offers. Sometimes we wander away from God's trail because we're just not paying attention. The activities of life become distracting to our relationship with God. When we lift our heads, we realize we are not on the trail anymore. We have simply stopped following and wandered away. On a trail ride, this is when the trail boss intervenes. Many times as a trail boss I had to physically grab the reins of another rider's horse and fight him back to the trail and into line. God is constantly grabbing our reins, and the Holy Spirit continually works to keep us in the true faith and on God's trail. Perhaps even now you have wandered away, and God is using this series to bring you back.

Unfortunately, there are also times when we have purposefully turned our horse away from our trail boss and the safety of His trail. We have considered His trail but decided to blaze one of our own. We might walk away from God for days, months, or even years, thinking that we have found our own way. But at the end of our trail, we find the same thing again and again: that we are lost. In these times, it is good to remember that our trail boss is also the Good Shepherd who "will seek the lost, and . . . bring back the strayed" (Ezekiel 34:16). He is not satisfied to have even one who is lost. What comfort it is that our trail boss, the Good Shepherd, will not leave us lost. Instead, He pursues us at great cost and brings us back to His trail.

Any discussion of trail riding would be incomplete without talking about the dangers of going first in the line. As the lead rider, the trail boss experiences the trail first. He must clear the trail of everything from thorns and thistles to wild animals. It's not unusual for the trail boss and his horse to finish the day with a few cuts and scrapes as a result of leading the way. But were it not for his work, the trail would be a perilous journey for all who followed. Likewise, God has led the way, sending His own Son to die on the cross and clear the path to everlasting life. Consider these familiar words from Isaiah. "He was wounded for our transgressions; He was crushed for our iniquities; upon Him was the chastisement that brought us peace, and with His stripes we are healed" (Isaiah 53:5). Our trail boss has been wounded with thorns, nails, and a spear for our transgressions. He bears the scars of being the first in line. He was cursed so that those who walk in His ways would be blessed.

The trail through life is not always an easy one. Because of our sinful flesh, there are times when we stumble and lose our way. Thank God we have a trail boss who goes before us, who seeks us when we are lost, and who restores us to His righteous path. Men, we have received forgiveness, life, and salvation from God our Father. Let us now be trail bosses in our own homes, leading our families to follow Him. To Him be all glory forever. Amen.

....

Thank God we have a trail boss who goes before us, who seeks us when we are lost, and who restores us to His righteous path.

Prayer: Lord Jesus Christ, thank You for freely choosing to rescue me from my sins. Help me each day to choose to follow You in spite of what may lie ahead, because I know You will lead me along the path of eternal life. In Your name I pray. Amen.

....

Monday

DAILY STUDY QUESTIONS
Psalm 128:1

1. What do you think it means to be blessed?

2. The "fear of the Lord" is a common phrase throughout the Bible. What does it look like when someone knows and lives by "the fear of the Lord"?

3. The psalmist connects blessing with walking in the Lord's ways. How does walking in God's ways bring blessing?

4. Scripture teaches us that our Lord is the Good Shepherd. Today, we've considered Him as the good trail boss. What other metaphors might be used to capture this aspect of God's provision and direction in your life?

5. What steps do you need to take today to bring your ways more in line with God's ways?

Psalm 128:2

You shall eat the fruit of the labor of your hands; you shall
be blessed, and it shall be well with you.

God's Agenda

Like two explorers clearing a trail through life's jungle, my wife, Becky, and I muddled our way through our first year of marriage. Doesn't that sound romantic? Two young people hand in hand, carving a path through life. For better, for worse, for richer, for poorer, in sickness and in health, to love and cherish . . . you know the rest. It was quite a setup Pastor Koch gave us, making us promise before God to never give up, even through the ups and downs marriage was sure to throw at us. Arguments about everything from the checkbook to the bathroom sink consumed our energy and our vocal chords. I'm sure the neighbors in our Chicago apartment complex often wondered if our wedded bliss would survive the first six months. In actuality, we were less like explorers and more like sculptors, chipping and chopping at each other, trying to create a spousal masterpiece.

We've been married nearly twenty years now, and apart from the obvious work God has done on both of us, there is one quality that has blessed our marriage more than any other: our sense of humor. Were it not for learning to laugh, the labor of making marriage work would have continued to be unbearable. This devotion is about God's agenda for life and extending His blessings at home and at work.

Nearly every one of us has attempted to provide food for our family by means of a garden. A man gains some satisfaction out of seeing the fruits of his labor providing sustenance for his family. I remember my dad planting tomatoes, radishes, and watermelons. Some years I remember the blessings we received at harvest time, but the labor of planting I remember a lot more. The apple doesn't fall far from the tree. At our house, my kids have also had to endure many years of planting the garden but only occasionally the harvesting of consumable fruits and vegetables. Some years it has been downright funny how bad I am at growing things. Of course, the hearty farmers among us have actually done this successfully. For the rest of us, simply planting a garden every spring will suffice as an adequate deterrent to becoming a farmer.

The psalmist's words "the fruit of the labor of your hands" do not mean that God requires each of us to labor at growing fruit. However, he does require us to labor at something. Paul told the Thessalonians, "If anyone is not willing to work, let him not eat" (2 Thessalonians 3:10). Unlike this verse from Paul, however, the psalmist shares a grace-filled version of these words, reminding us that God's blessings come to us in and through the labor of our hands. In light of this, why wouldn't we want to leave home every morning overcome with joy for the blessings of God soon to be showered upon us at work? Okay, I hope you sense the humor in the last sentence.

The truth is that in my own life I fail to even look for God's blessings when I'm at work. Rather, I get caught up with my own agenda for each day. Isn't it the same way for you?

Men, we forget that it is God who provides for our needs by blessing us with work and a paycheck. We forget that it is He who created our hands and our minds and equips us to serve Him. His agenda is the key to blessings in life.

Trusting God's agenda is part of the daily labor of our hands. Though we daily sin and fail to trust Him, we can rejoice that He has blessed us with forgiveness through Jesus' death on the cross. When you consider your life at home and at work, know that God's most important agenda item is that you have been washed in the blood of Jesus.

God's agenda is the same for us in work as in marriage. Becky and I began our marriage as sculptors, but we have labored to become explorers of His blessings in Christ, and He has taken our two agendas and made them one. God's one agenda is much more of a blessing than our individual agendas could ever be, and it's much more fun.

Shortly after we bought our first home, the fun began. I was excited to get busy planting a garden and taking care of things outside. I noticed that several trees in our yard were cherry trees. Being a lover of all things cherry, I was beside myself with the thought of the hundreds of fresh cherries that I would soon be picking. I hoped these would be Bing cherries.

Every morning before work, I would take my cup of coffee and walk through the yard to my cherry trees. There I would inspect them to make sure the birds hadn't begun to nibble on the small yellow fruits that were beginning to grow. As the summer progressed, Becky finally asked if I really thought those smallish-looking yellow things were Bing cherries? I actually had no proof that these were even cherry trees, but my answer was always "Yes, I'm pretty sure these are Bing cherries." Perhaps I was already in denial.

Late in July, the fruits began to turn red, but not the dark red I had expected and hoped for. When Becky realized there was no way these were going to be Bing cherries, she hatched her plan. She bought ten pounds of Bing cherries at the grocery store. Late one night she snuck out into the backyard, and by the light of the moon she glued the Bing cherries to my trees. As you can imagine, the next day I was ecstatic when I reached the trees and found that half of the fruit had finally turned the dark red color I had expected. The game was up when she couldn't keep a straight face long enough to ask me if there were any ripe cherries on the tree this morning. We had a great laugh together over breakfast, which included some wonderful Bing cherries, sort of from my trees.

May God richly bless your labor at home and at work today, and may you receive power to rejoice in His agenda for your life, especially that Jesus is your Savior.

When you consider your life at home and at work, know that God's most important agenda item is that you have been washed in the blood of Jesus.

Prayer: Heavenly Father, forgive me for demanding that You follow my agenda. Help me to rightly order my life at home, at work, at church, and in my community so that I might serve You in all that I do. I ask this for Jesus' sake. Amen.

Tuesday

DAILY STUDY QUESTIONS
Psalm 128:2

1. What sort of fruit have you been working to grow?

2. Does the happiness of harvest happen only once, or does God bring many harvests at certain points of your labor?

3. In what sense are all of the harvest times that we experience but foretastes of the ultimate harvest?

4. In what ways is it true that we are all beneficiaries of a "glued-on harvest" that was not of our own making?

5. How do you need to adjust your attitude toward work so that you begin to see it more fully as a gift from God that allows you to be a productive part of His creation?

Psalm 128:3

Your wife will be like a fruitful vine within your house; your
children will be like olive shoots around your table.

The Olsen Family Reunion

There is no good way to begin this devotion. I am at the same time embarrassed by my actions and proud of my resourcefulness in the following true story.

One afternoon, while traveling in Wisconsin, I took my family to a nice park for a picnic. Above the park's picnic pavilion hung a sign: Olsen Family Reunion (the name of the family has been changed to protect the innocent . . . and the guilty).

We found a nice quiet table away from the pavilion, and Becky opened the cooler to serve lunch, a nice big bowl of pasta salad. We had forgotten to pack forks, so I decided to walk to the Olsen family reunion and try to borrow a few. On the way, I talked with lots of members of the Olsen family. There were kids at the playground, men pitching horseshoes, women playing cards, and teenagers talking around the bed of a pickup truck. I thought the Olsen family seemed a lot like my own family. In the words of our psalm for today, it must have been a blessing for the older folks to see all of the olive shoots gathered to celebrate the family. I passed through a gathering of men on the porch and walked into the pavilion. This is when things began to get complicated.

There was no one in the kitchen, but I did see several packages of plastic forks. I looked around for an Olsen family member, but seeing none, I decided to just take five forks and sneak out the back door. I know what you're thinking: crime doesn't pay . . . he's going to get caught. When I turned to go, three junior high girls walked into the kitchen. I asked them, "Can I take a few forks?" When the girls walked past me without saying a word, I had a junior high flashback. I faked a smile and headed out of the dance—I mean the kitchen.

Just as I got through the door, an elderly woman with grey hair and a cane met me from the other side. She was wearing lots of lipstick, and I was afraid she was going to kiss me, thinking I was a long-lost nephew. What she did next made me think I was in real trouble. Laughing, she pulled me out of the kitchen by my arm and shoved me to the edge of the pavilion porch. On the way, she let out a yell in my ear, "Get up there, they're taking the men's picture." This is the moment when the slow motion begins in my memory. Sure enough, situated in front of me on the porch steps were dozens and dozens of Olsen family grandpas, dads, and sons, all posing for the Olsen family picture.

Since I'm not an Olsen, I had two options: one, admit to stealing five plastic forks and ask for leniency; two, stand there, look at the camera, and smile. The decision was quite easy. Seeing as the picture was just seconds from being taken, and since there were so many men in the Olsen family, I doubted they would notice just one more person. So, I gave them the biggest Olsen family grin I could muster.

With all of the wives and daughters standing in front taking pictures, I thought for sure someone would notice that I wasn't an Olsen. Surprisingly, several people said hi to me as if they knew who I was. I'm actually honored that they thought I was one of them.

The psalmist in today's verse describes a family like the Olsens. A family that is beautiful like a fruitful vine. My wife really tries to be like this to me, but I am sad to admit that I don't always care for her like a gardener should care for his most precious vine. I see how my children are like tender shoots, sprouting forth from my roots, but there have been many times that I have been a poor example for them of a fruitful tree.

What about you? God has appointed you to tend your family like a gardener tends his garden. You are to be leading your family on behalf of God, and He promises to bless you in that endeavor. In his Small Catechism, Dr. Martin Luther said, "As the head of the family should teach them in a simple way to his household." Do you ask God for the simple words and the opportunity to study the basics of faith with your wife and children? Most important to your leadership role is believing in your own heart that Jesus died on the cross for your sins. Take courage. You are forgiven. Through His death, you have been given life. You have been set free in order to proclaim God's riches.

We have a great gift in the cross of Christ, Jesus. As husbands and fathers serving on His behalf, we are guided by the Holy Spirit as we tell our families this Good News. The task is not to be looked upon lightly, and it is not meant for us to attempt alone. He has given us the Comforter and His Church to walk beside us.

So, are you wondering if I ended up getting caught? After the photo, I said hi to a few Olsens, and then I hoofed it around the porch and headed back to my family. Out of breath, I had quite a story for Becky and the kids when I arrived at our picnic table. I do wonder sometimes if the Olsen family ever asks who the tall guy with the big grin in the back row is . . . and what is he hiding behind his back?

God bless you today as you represent Him with your fruitful vine and your olive shoots. I pray that you point them to Jesus and His cross. Amen.

As husbands and fathers serving on His behalf, we are guided by the Holy Spirit as we tell our families this Good News.

Prayer: Dear God, through Baptism You grafted me into Your true Vine, my Savior, Jesus Christ. Forgive me for the times I have not tended my family as I should. Help me to serve them better, as You richly nourish me with Your grace. In Jesus' name. Amen.

Wednesday

DAILY STUDY QUESTIONS
Psalm 128:3

1. If you told your wife (or you mother) that she was like a "fruitful vine," how would it be received?

2. Why is the agricultural imagery particularly apt with reference to raising a family?

3. What responsibility does a father have for the care of his vine and his olive plants (no disrespect toward wife or children intended)?

4. It is quite interesting that even in the time of the psalmist, the family is pictured gathered around the table. What is it about the shared family table that evokes a sense of unity and blessing?

5. What specific tasks of family cultivation need your attention today?

Psalm 128:4

Behold, thus shall the man be blessed who fears the LORD.

The Fear of the Lord

As a child, there was a seat at my kitchen table where only my dad would sit. Like piglets around a feeding trough, six children jockeyed for position around the edges of that table. If anyone dared move to the head of the table, the others would squeal, "You're in dad's spot!" My dad ruled our house from his chair at the kitchen table. He always seemed to have wise words and an educated perspective. That seat reminds me of God's position in our lives. As the author of life itself, God has a perspective that we cannot fathom. It can be downright frightening, what God knows about each of us.

Since the title of this series is *Blessed Is the Man*, I'll make the assumption that Psalm 128:4 could be an important verse. I want God to bless my life. So, am I reading this verse right to say that all I need to do is fear the Lord? The fear of the Lord is a good thing. Verse 4 says so, right? But just when this fear the Lord thing sounds simple, I hear what God said to the Israelites just after giving them the Ten Commandments. "Fear the LORD your God, you and your son and your son's son, by keeping all His statutes and His commandments" (Deuteronomy 6:2). Ouch! Does that mean what I think it means? Is the fear of the Lord keeping the Ten Commandments? This could be problematic because I know me, and I probably know you too. Sin has plagued us since . . . well, since we can remember being able to remember. Is it even possible to really fear the Lord?

There is even ample evidence to prove that I was born with a sinning problem. One early memory of it is from when I was nine years old, helping my dad with our church pancake breakfast. It was 1976, the two hundredth anniversary of the nation, and I think it was the hundredth anniversary of the pancake breakfast. At the end of one of the hallways was a coatrack on wheels. When no one was watching, I rode that coatrack like a skateboard as fast as I could up and down the hallway. Along with the thrill of pretending to be A. J. Foyt, I found an added bonus when two Bicentennial silver dollars fell from the top of the coatrack.

Here is where I wish I could say that I was torn between doing right and doing wrong. The truth is I put the coins in my pocket as fast as I could. When the breakfast ended, one man announced that he had lost two silver dollars. I remember my dad specifically asking, "Did you see any coins near that coatrack in the hall?" "Nope!" I replied.

When we got home, I headed straight to my bedroom. As I took off my church pants, the coins fell out of my pocket and landed on the floor, rolling to a stop under my bed. My siblings heard the whirling ring the coins made as they came to rest. My fate was sealed when they yelled, "Money!" and ran into my room. My dad was quite upset when he found out the coins under my bed were the same ones the gentleman at church had lost. This was certainly one of those times I had good reason to fear my father.

God requires that we fear Him and keep His Ten Commandments. Jesus affirms the eternal consequences of fearing the Lord in Luke 12:5, saying, "Fear Him who, after He has killed, has authority to cast into hell." To put it bluntly, we could say, "I want to keep the Ten Commandments because I want to go to heaven." Men, this statement creates a major problem in all of our lives. We are sinners, unable by our own reason or strength to fear God and keep His Commandments. We are unable to receive the blessings reserved for those who fear God.

Thankfully, our Lord does not leave us in this lost and condemned state. Rather, He has provided a mediator to fear God on our behalf, one who suffered the consequences of our sin on the cross. Jesus has taken our sinful hearts, unable to fear God, and has given us new hearts. He has taken our fear of God's wrath and given us the freedom to know God without fear. In Luke 12:6–7, Jesus continues His teaching on fear, telling us how much the Father loves us: "Are not five sparrows sold for two pennies. . . . Even the hairs of your head are all numbered. Fear not; you are of more value than many sparrows." Though we are still in awe of God's authority over life and death, Jesus' work on the cross has eliminated our fear of God's wrath. Our fear is no longer directed at whether we will go to heaven or hell. Rather, our fear of God is like being in awe of His wonderful acts, especially His work of redemption.

This brings me back to my kitchen table as a child. In some respects, we feared my dad's position at our table. However, it was more like we marveled at the decisions and announcements he made from that seat. "You're grounded!" "We're moving." "Your mother is going to have a baby." "Grandpa has died." This fear of my father and his seat at the table was not so much like being afraid of him as it was being in awe of the authority he had in our lives.

You have received the blessings of salvation through Jesus. You have freely received because Jesus has perfectly feared God on your behalf. Your response is to marvel at His goodness and grace. He has removed your fear of God's wrath and punishment. Be filled with the joy. This truly is the fear of the Lord, to live as one who is redeemed and free from fear.

You have received the blessings of salvation through Jesus. You have freely received because Jesus has perfectly feared God on your behalf.

Prayer: Heavenly Father, show me my sin with Your Law, and assure me of Your forgiveness through Your Son. Give me confidence in all that I do, as I rest in the awe and wonder and majesty of Your grace. In Jesus' name. Amen.

Thursday

DAILY STUDY QUESTIONS
Psalm 128:4

1. What was your relationship with your father like? Did it include an element of fear?

2. How is it possible to dearly love, profoundly respect, and genuinely fear someone all at the same time?

3. The author rightly notes that his father provoked awe in the children of the family simply by virtue of his "seat." What roles do relationship and authority play in our understanding of where we fit within God's creation?

4. What are some ways, recently, that you have been trying to take God's seat at the table?

5. How is it true that the only possible way to truly fear God is through faith in Christ?

Psalm 128:5-6

The LORD bless you from Zion! May you see the prosperity of Jerusalem all the days of your life! May you see your children's children! Peace be upon Israel!

The Wake of the Gospel

A few years back, we lived near a lake just outside of Nashville, Tennessee. Hardly a day went by that we didn't drive over the dam and see people boating, fishing, skiing, or just hanging out near the water. The kids always wanted to go spend the weekend at "our" lake. One summer I finally gave in, and we went camping.

Each morning of our campout, the kids and I would walk to the water and go fishing just before sunrise. The first morning, my first cast was kindly retrieved by Dorothy, our German shorthair. After replacing the chewed-up bobber, I prepared to cast again, only to notice that Kohlbe, our black labrador, was swimming after a family of ducks. The mother duck knew exactly what she was doing as she splashed the water, leaving a wake that led Kolhbe out into the middle of the lake. Kohlbe was relentless. She would not come back until the mother duck was completely out of sight. We decided that the dogs were not going fishing with us again. Too exhausted to continue fishing, we went back to bed.

The second morning, it was quiet and serene for our fishing adventure. Like a mirror, the lake reflected the image of the trees and hills on the other side. We made our casts and prepared to haul in the big one. In the distance was a boat, and we heard the quiet hum of the motor. The hum turned to a low rumble as the boat made its way up the channel. Then, as it turned toward us, the sound became more like the roar of a jet engine. Passing just offshore, the wake of the boat splashed water into our tackle box, tipped our can of worms, and tangled our lines. The waves washed over the rocks and soaked the kids' shoes. I was in the water deep enough to have water up to my waist. Our lines were in knots, our worms were escaping, and my shorts were wet. For the second morning in a row, we had a good laugh and decided fishing was just too much work.

It became more evident throughout the weekend that nothing can travel in water without leaving a wake. Boats, dogs, ducks, and even bugs left a wake. The waves traveled through the water all the way to the shore.

In our Scripture passage, the blessing of God is the prosperity of Jerusalem. For us, prosperity lies in the blessings of the kingdom of God, everything that Jesus has accomplished on the cross. We are blessed to see this prosperity as it moves through our lives like the wake of a boat moves across the lake. Were it not for the devil, the world, and our sinful flesh, the sound of the Gospel waves lapping at the shoreline would be like the sound of a beautiful symphony.

As followers of Christ, we see and feel the wake of the Gospel. But all too often there are competing waves on the lake. We are attacked with waves of sin, and our weakness leaves us overcome by the devil's schemes.

Try this experiment. On a calm day, throw a rock onto the glass-like surface of a lake. Watch as the wake from the splash flows back to the shore. Try the same experiment during a thunderstorm. The wind and the raindrops hitting the surface of the water make it nearly impossible to follow the wake. Likewise, it is easy to follow the wake of the Gospel through the good times in life. But add a few sick days, some financial struggles, a death in the family, and our own sinfulness, and we have a recipe for disaster on the open water.

The shoreline of my own life is riddled with shipwrecks and near drowning experiences, the results of my own sinfulness and failure to follow in God's wake. Like Peter walking on the lake to Jesus, I want to follow, but I find myself sinking in the storms of life, doubting that God will rescue me. The words of Jesus cut me to the quick, "O you of little faith, why did you doubt?" (Matthew 14:31).

It is clear that because of our own sinfulness, God has every right to leave us abandoned on the shoreline. Like my labrador paddling aimlessly with no chance of catching the ducks, you could spend your life lost and without hope for rescue. But at the cross, Jesus provided for your salvation. His wake washed over you in the waters of Baptism. In this heavenly exchange, the old Adam was drowned and you were born anew. Now you are holy, and as you go through life, you also will leave a wake. Your wake is the message of the Gospel, which you share with others. If you are a Sunday School teacher or youth leader, your students feel the wake. When one of your students reaches out to a hurting friend at school because of a lesson you taught them, someone else feels the wake. If you're a father, your children feel the wake daily. Many people feel the wake when you encourage your kids to live out their faith and share it with others. The Apostle Paul summarizes the flowing wake of the Gospel in this way, "In the whole world [the Gospel] is bearing fruit and growing—as it also does among you, since the day you heard it and understood the grace of God in truth" (Colossians 1:6). The wake of the Gospel is moving through the world as the Word of God is proclaimed from the lips of believers.

Indeed, you are blessed to see the prosperity of the Gospel as it is proclaimed in your own life and in the lives of those around you. May this prosperity bring you great joy, and may the Holy Spirit keep you following the wake of our Lord and Savior, Jesus.

....

Now you are holy, and as you go through life, you also will leave a wake. Your wake is the message of the Gospel, which you share with others.

Prayer: Holy Spirit, when my sinful flesh draws me away from Jesus, bring me to repentance. Help me to turn away from life's distractions so I look to Jesus only. Cause His light to shine through me to my family, friends, and co-workers. In Jesus' name. Amen.

....

Friday

DAILY STUDY QUESTIONS
Psalm 128:5–6

1. What sort of "wakes" have caught you this past week? Are there certain people in your life who seem to kick up an especially powerful and disruptive wake?

2. What sort of wake have you been leaving during the last few days? Have people caught in your wake been blessed or been left indifferent or even hurt?

3. What comes to mind when you hear the word *Zion*? What do Zion, Jerusalem, and Israel have to do with you?

4. Why should a man have great joy in seeing his grandchildren?

5. What does it mean to you to have peace?

Week Five

PSALM 128

The 128th psalm is a psalm of comfort in which the estate of marriage is splendidly praised. Marriage partners are given this great comfort: they should not look only at the trouble, work, discouragement, and discomfort they feel and experience in marriage, but rather look at the gracious will of God toward them, that their station and life are a gracious creation of God and are blessed by Him. Therefore, marriage is dear to Him, and He gives it much more happiness and blessing than discomfort, if one only believes and adapts oneself to marriage and faithfully remains within it. Thus in the beginning and middle of the psalm it says, "everyone who fears the Lord . . ." When the godless go astray, on the other hand, it is no surprise.

– Martin Luther

GROUP BIBLE STUDY
(Questions and answers are on pp. 186–88.)

1. Tell about a time when you felt especially blessed? What was it that made that a blessed time?

2. What is the difference between being blessed and being fortunate or lucky?

3. We are told (v. 1) to walk in God's ways. Are His ways the same for every one of us, or does He have a different way for each of us? What's the same, and what's different?

4. Is the work you do (at home or at your job) a curse or a blessing? How does God want us to understand our work (consider Genesis 2:15 and Ecclesiastes 9:10)?

5. If we live in a broken world, and if sin pollutes and perverts everything, making our existence a vale of tears, how can a Christian man ever justify feeling happy?

6. How does a biblical view of the place and importance of the family differ from the view of the culture around us?

OKAY TO COPY THIS PAGE.   134

7. What is a father's responsibility toward his wife and children? Why is it important to recognize a father's responsibility as much more than providing a roof overhead and food on the table?

8. Besides being indicative of long life, what is the blessing of living to see your "children's children"? How might this, in some circumstances actually be a painful and unpleasant thing? What do your actions now have to do with which experience you have?

9. Zion, Jerusalem, and Israel do not have as much relevance for us as they did for those who used this psalm in the days of the Davidic kingdom and even down to the time of Jesus and Paul. What meaning might we take from these names today?

10. Decide on one thing you will do today at work or in your home that will enact in your life God's way of blessedness.

Week Six

Psalm 139:1–12

[1] O LORD, You have searched me and known me!

[2] You know when I sit down and when I rise up;
You discern my thoughts from afar.

[3] You search out my path and my lying down
and are acquainted with all my ways.

[4] Even before a word is on my tongue,
behold, O LORD, You know it altogether.

[5] You hem me in, behind and before,
and lay Your hand upon me.

[6] Such knowledge is too wonderful for me;
it is high; I cannot attain it.

[7] Where shall I go from Your Spirit?
Or where shall I flee from Your presence?

[8] If I ascend to heaven, You are there!
If I make my bed in Sheol, You are there!

[9] If I take the wings of the morning
and dwell in the uttermost parts of the sea,
I can hear them through the walls for me.

[10] even there Your hand shall lead me,
and Your right hand shall hold me.

[11] If I say, "Surely the darkness shall cover me,
and the light about me be night,"

[12] even the darkness is not dark to You;
the night is bright as the day,
for darkness is as light with You.

Gary Dunker

Psalm 139:1–4

O Lord, You have searched me and known me! You know
when I sit down and when I rise up; You discern my thoughts
from afar. You search out my path and my lying down and
are acquainted with all my ways. Even before a word is on my
tongue, behold, O Lord, You know it altogether.

Check the Czech

Growing up in a small Nebraska town in the 1950s had its advantages. In those days, everyone in town knew your parents. No matter what you did away from home, your parents knew about it before you arrived home. There were also Saturday nights. Everyone went to town on Saturday nights. As a child, I passed many street corners filled with "old people" talking in their native German or Czechoslovakian. The verse "Before a word is on my tongue, behold, O Lord, You know it altogether" (Psalm 139:4) held no meaning back then. It does now as I think back to some fifty years ago.

For years, my uncle and I were inseparable. Although he was my father's youngest brother, he was only two years older than me. My father, mother, and I often spent time at my grandparents' home, where my uncle lived. Frequently, other cousins or neighborhood children would join us for a game of hide-and-seek in the dark. Occasionally, someone in the group would relay a new swear word they had overheard. One particular night, the words were Czech. We repeated them until we had pronounced them "just right." After a few minutes of practice, we'd giggle and scurry off to some other childhood adventure, such as reliving an episode of *The Lone Ranger* or *Peter Gunn* we'd seen on the television.

As weeks passed, our little group continued to meet. Using our new vocabulary became second nature to us. Knowing the meaning of the words only heightened the experience. We knew we were talking like adults and thought that only our group and a few "old people" knew their meaning.

One day, workers began excavating the vacant lot east of my grandparents' house. The resulting dirt mound became the site of enthusiastic games of King on the Mountain. Losers cursed in Czech under their breath as they slid off the top. Sometimes a dirt clod fight erupted after King on the Mountain. In this 1950s equivalent of a paintball game, one team attacked the mountain under a hail of dirt clods. The sting of dirt clods achieving their target always prompted an angry outburst of our favorite Czech profanity. Among my circle of friends, using swear words became second nature. Anytime something failed to go as planned, out they came. We were always so careful not to let an adult hear us, because we knew trouble awaited us if they heard. "Don't tell anyone, especially your mom and dad," we admonished each other at evening's end.

One summer afternoon when I was eight, everything changed. No matter how carefully I tried to keep from swearing in front of my parents, the words were bound to slip out. I remember coming in from play to ask my mother for a snack. She said, "Wash up first." Then out they flew—two little words I had concealed from her for three months. Her face was filled with shock and horror. Her brows furrowed. Her lips pursed. Her momentary stutter gave way to "You didn't think I knew what those words meant, did you?" I shook my head in stunned disbelief. I had no idea that she knew their meaning. How could she? She wasn't an "old person." For a moment, time stood still. She knew! "I never want to hear you say those words again," she demanded.

She reached for the bar of soap that always sat near the kitchen sink. Some may say that having your mouth washed out with soap is cruel. In my younger days, I would have agreed. Now, I happen to believe that I deserved a punishment far more severe. For months on end, I had flippantly taken the Lord's name in vain. I thought only a few people, and certainly not my mother, knew what the words meant. My mother's response shocked me as much as my flippant words shocked her. She responded with swift discipline. She sought no explanation, for I had none to offer her.

The psalmist says of God, "You have searched me and known me" (v. 1). He knows "when I sit down and when I rise up," and He perceives "my thoughts from afar" (v. 2). I hide nothing from God for He is "acquainted with all my ways" (v. 3). Just as my words deeply hurt my mother, they had already hurt our Lord, for "before a word is on my tongue, behold, O Lord, you know it altogether" (v. 4). Our misuse of the Lord's name earns God's full-blown wrath. We stand accused. God's Law condemns us. The opening four verses of Psalm 139 strike fear in our hearts. God knows us so intimately, it's scary.

Still, we know that our all-powerful yet forgiving God is "slow to anger and abounding in steadfast love" (Psalm 145:8). By faith, we cling to God's promises. Paul puts it this way: "Christ redeemed us from the curse of the law by becoming a curse for us—for it is written, 'Cursed is everyone who is hanged on a tree'" (Galatians 3:13). Indeed, "the LORD is good to all; and His mercy is over all that he has made" (Psalm 145:9). Because of His mercy through Christ, we do not receive the punishment we deserve for our sins. Jesus took on our sins and suffered for them fully on His cross.

Have you recently used the Lord's name in vain, whether intentionally or unintentionally? Then confess it, my brother. Don't wait until someone like your mom, your wife, or your daughter brings it to your attention. Know that the price for your words was not your mom's bar of soap but the very body and blood of Your Savior. His words from the cross—"Father, forgive them"—cleanse you in body and soul. In thanksgiving for your cleansing, you can join the psalmist by praying, "My mouth will speak in praise of the LORD. Let every creature praise His holy name forever and ever" (Psalm 145:21).

Know that the price for your words was not your mom's bar of soap but the very body and blood of Your Savior.

Prayer: Lord Jesus Christ, help me to control my tongue so that I use it to build up, not to tear down. Let my voice be used for blessing, not for cursing, so that others, too, might be drawn to praise Your saving name. Amen.

Monday

DAILY STUDY QUESTIONS
Psalm 139:1–4

1. What are some of the thoughts and words that have been on your mind lately and that you'd rather *not* be known to God?

2. How does it strike you to realize that God is even more aware of those thoughts and words than you are?

3. No doubt you've seen that look of disbelief, "shock and horror," on the face of an adult reacting to a sin you have done. How do you think God reacts to that same sin?

4. How does God's complete knowing of you convict you?

5. How does God's complete knowing of you comfort you?

Psalm 139:5-6

You hem me in, behind and before, and lay Your hand upon me. Such knowledge is too wonderful for me; it is high; I cannot attain it.

Hemmed In

I am an avid Nebraska football fan, so when I think of someone being "hemmed in," I usually think of our quarterback being protected by Husker defensive linemen. Now that image isn't exactly what we read about in today's verses. But God did place His hand on us in Baptism. And He hemmed us in too. Sure, He didn't do so using a 6-foot 5-inch, 320-pound football player, but He hemmed us in with His all-powerful grace. Do you recall the story in the Book of Job, the one where Satan approached God? The devil sought God's permission to tempt Job by asking Him to remove His "hedge" from around Job and his family (Job 1:10). God removed His protection from all but Job and His wife, and Satan went to work. Job lost sons, daughters, and numerous possessions, only to regain them again at the end of the story. But God never "unhemmed" Job, who despite the tragedy in his life, clung to Him in faith.

A year removed from college, my wife and I loaded our meager possessions into the largest rental truck we could afford. After a year of working on the kill floor of a beef processing plant, we pointed our truck south 180 miles, three hours from family and friends. Much thought had gone into leaving one job for another while halving my salary. My education had prepared me to be a teacher, and my dream of imparting knowledge was very much alive. I still remember seeing my youngest brother in tears, his image reflected in the side mirrors as we drove away.

Several weeks earlier, when I was interviewing for jobs, my wife and I discovered that the main access road several miles northwest of our destination had been closed. We were forced to take a detour so that we could enter the city from the southwest. A flashing caution light marked our turn. North- and south-bound traffic slowed before proceeding through the intersection or turning either east or west. A flashing red light stopped east- and west-bound traffic. For the next three years, the orange flashing lights signaled to us that home was only eight miles away.

As it happened, our landlords were also our neighbors. At twenty-three and my wife at twenty-one, we were only a few years older than our landlords' oldest child. Their children attended the Catholic high school. I taught speech and dramatics in the public high school. With school in session, I often arrived at school at 7:15 a.m. and left again at 4 p.m. That schedule changed when I directed plays and musicals. During those times, I returned to school at 7 p.m. and arrived back home about 9:30 p.m. (Several years after I left teaching for a career in radio broadcasting, my accountant wife estimated my salary to direct plays and musicals at twenty-five cents per hour.) Could I see then how God had "hemmed me in"? Not really. Sure, I believed God existed, but I really gave it no further thought.

If I had no extracurricular assignments, we'd drive "home" for the weekend, often returning much later than we intended. The flashing orange lights served as reminders that our return trip was nearly over. One Sunday night, we began our return trip much later than usual. I don't remember the reason for leaving at 9 p.m. instead of the customary 7 p.m. I do remember that we first noticed the flashing orange lights in the distance sometime around midnight. Nearing the intersection from the north, my peripheral vision caught the reflection of headlights approaching to my left. You probably recall that a flashing red light at an intersection means that a driver is supposed to stop. As my wife and I neared the intersection, a verbal debate began, one of those rare instances when I have been right:

"He's not slowing down," I said.

"But he has a stoplight," she countered.

"You know it and I know it, but I don't think he does. He's going too fast to stop," I replied.

"He'll stop. . . ."

Those words barely left my wife's lips when I slammed on the brakes and skidded to a halt, the nose of my car some two feet into the intersection. To this day, I'm not sure if the other driver saw us or not. All I know is that he raced through the intersection. Had I not stopped, his car would have broadsided ours, probably killing us instantly. For several minutes afterwards, my wife and I huddled together in tears. We were too terrified to record his license plate number. As the car's taillights disappeared into the night, we estimated its speed at over ninety miles per hour. We became very aware of God's hemming us in that night—by His gracious providential care.

We could also say that we have been hemmed in because of what Jesus did for us on the cross. Jesus took the hits we deserved on the front line of Calvary. Without

Him we'd be looking at nothing but turf. He was beaten, bruised, and battered, but what was a bloody, deadly defeat was really His victory. He proved He was the winner by His resurrection. Knowing that we're hemmed in because of Jesus, regardless of what we face, helps us to recognize and to give Him thanks for His daily care in our lives.

I still shudder recalling how God spared my wife and me from certain death. While too much to comprehend, we can nevertheless give thanks to God for His mercy. A friend of mine puts God's hemming in into perspective, saying, "Because of Jesus Christ, we do not receive the punishment we deserve, leaving us to wonder how many times God's mercy spared us from pain and suffering." Men, give thanks to God for hemming you in from eternal death through Jesus' victory on the cross. And remember also how God protects you and your family daily by His grace.

Jesus took the hits we deserved on the front line of Calvary. Without Him, we'd be looking at nothing but turf.

Prayer: Heavenly Father, You send Your holy angels to protect me from harm and danger. Thank You for giving me Your Son, whose death and resurrection assure me of Your merciful and caring hand. In Jesus' name I pray. Amen.

Tuesday

DAILY STUDY QUESTIONS
Psalm 139:5-6

1. Recall a time when God's "protecting hedge" was dramatically and especially evident. How did that incident affect your faith and your overall attitude toward life?

2. Why is it that during ordinary days we may be lulled into indifference or even doubt regarding God's presence and protective care?

3. What is it about verse 5 that makes David stop and marvel at the implications of his thoughts about God?

4. Why is it important to stop at times and remember the astounding greatness and surpassing power, wisdom, and wonder of our God?

5. What danger might there be in becoming too comfortable with God and forgetting about His breathtaking—no, heart-stopping—might, authority, and holiness?

Psalm 139:7-8

Where shall I go from Your Spirit? Or where shall I flee from
Your presence? If I ascend to heaven, You are there! If I make
my bed in Sheol, You are there!

God's Special Child

God blessed me and my wife with two daughters. Both were born healthy. So, years later when I made my way into a children's intensive care unit, I didn't know what to expect. My new grandson came into the world six weeks early, weighing just over four pounds. When I arrived at the ICU, a nurse guided me to a sink where I washed with antibacterial soap and donned a surgical mask before joining his parents. Lying among a host of monitors, a tiny figure attached to an oversized head caught my attention. In many cases of spina bifida, fluid causes the baby's head to swell. In my grandson's case, abnormal head growth had led to his premature delivery. Monitors recorded every function of his tiny body. I noticed the name *Dathin* handwritten on a piece of paper Scotch taped to the side of his bed. His mom and dad had combined David and Nathan to come up with his name.

Spina bifida begins early in pregnancy, often before a woman knows she is expecting. In some cases, the bones of the spine do not form properly around the spinal cord. In the United States, spina bifida remains one of the most common birth defects. Statistically, of four million babies born, fifteen hundred to two thousand of these births involve some form of spina bifida. In my grandson's case, doctors tell us that the wound in his back remains one of the most severe they've ever seen. Most likely, Dathin will never walk and will face numerous operations that doctors hope will reshape his misshapen spine. Dathin's spine forms a *z* instead of the customary vertical line.

In Psalm 139, one of my grandson's biblical namesakes asks, "Where can I go from Your Spirit? Or where shall I flee from Your presence?" (v. 7). Sometimes, as sinful human beings, we ask instead, "God, where are You? How could You let this happen?" I must honestly tell you, questions like these often accompany the birth of a special needs child. How easily we see hopelessness when face-to-face with situations beyond our control. For me, if ever a situation permitted such questioning, the birth of Dathin was it. Yet I never heard these words escape the lips of my daughter or son-in-law. Where do we find God's presence in my grandson's story? After all, David notes, "If I ascend to heaven, You [God] are there; if I make my bed in Sheol, You are there" (v. 8). Can we find God in seemingly godless situations?

The poem "Footsteps" presents an interesting premise. A man dies and goes to heaven. There his life passes before him as footprints in the sand. He observes two sets of footprints during normal times, expressing his relationship with God, but only one set during times of trouble. Disappointed that God abandoned him during troubled times, the man questions God. "My dear child," God answers, "you see only one set of footprints during troubled times because those are the times I carried you." My family willingly concedes that God has carried us through troubled times. We find His footprints everywhere as we look back on Dathin's short lifetime. Let me put a few of God's footprints before you.

A routine examination of my daughter's amniotic fluid led to the discovery of my grandson's enlarged head. Early in my daughter's pregnancy, physicians knew Dathin had spina bifida and his special delivery was coordinated and planned. By God's hand, a prominent neurosurgeon attended Dathin immediately after his birth. This surgeon inspected Dathin's nerves and worked to seal the massive wound in his back. An out-of-state neonatal nurse with extensive training in spina bifida cases "happened" to be on staff at the hospital to lead Dathin's care team. Throughout Dathin's six-month hospital stay, a wonderful team of nurses oversaw his recovery. Members of our church and family provided prayers, meals, hospital visits, childcare, and gasoline as daily visits continued unendingly. A special Easter breakfast raised additional funds to offset medical expenses.

Almost immediately after Dathin's birth, my son-in-law began hanging Scripture verses in Dathin's room. Anyone who visited could not help but see God's Word. When the hospital offered Internet Care Pages, my son-in-law chronicled each day and selected a Bible verse to accompany his words. Often the time stamp on his Internet posting read 2 a.m. Truly, God's footprints were evident. His almighty presence granted safety during daily hundred-mile round trips in every imaginable weather.

As I type this devotional, Dathin is at home with his mom, dad, and older brother and sister. He weighs nearly eighteen pounds. While he remains on oxygen, he is allowed time to breathe on his own a few hours each day. Recent surgery to repair a defective shunt controlling spinal fluid went well. He came home with a brand new rattle in his hand, an anonymous gift from someone who cared for him. His father writes, "There is no doubt that God has a plan for all of us and He will fulfill it for His greater good."

How easily we overlook God's footprints in our lives. Instead of trusting His Word that He cares for everything about us, we look only on our seeming misfortune. When the sin of doubt blurs our vision, we only see the clouds of despair.

Yet, echoing the psalmist, Paul explains that God "put His seal on us and given us His Spirit in our hearts as a guarantee" (2 Corinthians 1:22). His "seal of ownership" came to us in Baptism. With water and Word, He laid claim to us. This is a living promise, ensured by Christ's cross and now-empty tomb. I have seen this promise lived out many times since Dathin's birth. Jesus says, "I am with you always, to the end of the age" (Matthew 28:20). As God's baptized children, there's no place that you or I can go without God being there too. And wherever Dathin goes, God our heavenly Father is already there.

....

With water and Word, He laid claim to us. This is a living promise, ensured by Christ's cross and now-empty tomb.

Prayer: Dear Lord, You richly shower Your blessings on me day by day. Help all of Your children who need Your special care and bless them each day until we rest in Your eternal presence forever. In Jesus' name I pray. Amen.

....

Wednesday

DAILY STUDY QUESTIONS
Psalm 139:7–8

1. Recall a time when it might have seemed as if God were not present in your circumstances. What indications of His presence were there in spite of the immediate evidence?

2. Have you ever tried to run from God? How did it go?

3. Is there anything especially striking about David's claim in verse 8?

4. How is the idea of God with us even in Sheol particularly pertinent for Christian believers?

5. What connection is there between Baptism and the promise of God's presence in life and in death?

Psalm 139:9–10

If I take the wings of the morning and dwell in the uttermost parts of the sea, even there Your hand shall lead me, and Your right hand shall hold me.

His Right Hand

My wife might say that *fan* does not cover my passion for football or for one major college football team in particular. To her, *fanatic* might come closer. We spent a few years living in southeast Kansas, far away from my beloved Nebraska Cornhuskers. Many Saturday afternoons I could be found holding a radio antenna so that I could listen to a station hundreds of miles away covering the play-by-play. No electric appliance (including the vacuum cleaner) was permitted to run during games, because the static interfered with my hearing the game. I often sat cross-legged on the bed, holding the antenna, letting go only to report scoring drives or retell some spectacular play. My game-day ritual remained the same; I tuned in about an hour before kickoff and listened throughout the game and every post-game show. But in 1993, we returned to Nebraska, and I didn't need the radio any more. Living in Lincoln, I was able to see nearly every home game!

Today's psalm mentions God's right hand. You may be thinking, *Where's he going with this devotion?* Please bear with me for a moment, and I'll connect the dots for you. Throughout history, a man's right hand symbolized mercy and justice. David reminds us that no matter where the faithful go, God goes with them; His right hand upholds and cares for them. God's mercy and justice never fail.

In football, we need a group of men to enforce the rules of the game. We call them referees. These men monitor the game clock and scoreboard; they stand among the players and watch for infractions. When they see one, they throw yellow flags onto the playing field and walk off the appropriate penalties. Players and spectators alike trust the judgment of these officials. They administer a form of human justice with which we may or may not agree. I'll use a recent game to illustrate my point. In doing so, I want you to understand that I am in no way questioning the officiating. Although I root for Nebraska, my seats are far away from the playing field, and I am not seeing the game through the unbiased eyes of an official on the field of play.

On this particular game day, the opposing team began a drive about three-quarters of the way through the third quarter. Aided by two pass interference calls on our defense, they arrived at our three-yard line. On first down, our defense rushed the quarterback, dropping him for a loss. A second sack followed. On third down the running back tried the right side, but our defense knocked the ball free. A Nebraska play recovered the fumble. My daughter sitting next to me began to text message her sister in Kansas with the news "We recovered a . . . "—she stopped as the head referee announced, "The previous play is under review." This is not the announcement a stadium filled with 84,000 red-clad Nebraska fans wants to hear. What followed, they liked even less. "Upon further review, there was no fumble. The running back's knee touched the ground prior to the fumble." "Fourth down!" the referee shouted as fans expressed their displeasure. I must admit that my voice was among them. Sitting in the north stadium, the opposite end of where the play occurred, I still cried out at the injustice done. The third quarter ended before the fourth down took place. Both teams huddled around their coaches and then moved to the north end of the field to resume play. An extremely vocal crowd greeted the defense, urging them to avenge the previous surmised "bad call."

The opposition broke their huddle at the thirty-yard line. They trailed by several touchdowns; a field goal's three points meant little. They needed a touchdown. Three receivers went to the left side of the formation and two to the right, with no running backs in the backfield. The quarterback dropped back to pass. The ball spiraled from his hands. He hit the turf unable to see that a defensive back stood where the quarterback thought his wide receiver should be, resulting in an interception at the three-yard line. Our defensive back weaved in and out of traffic before an opposing wide receiver back tackled him at our twenty-five. The partisan crowd collectively rose to its feet to signal "First down!" High-fives followed with such vigor that someone new to Memorial Stadium might have thought that the crowd single-handedly made the interception and blocked ahead of the defensive back, all in one motion. Then the crowd seated itself while murmuring aloud how our defense had risen to the occasion. Our defense overcame the injustice an official caused with his ruling: "After further review, there is no fumble." Now, I heard myself shouting, "After further review, the play stands as called: first and ten Nebraska!"

Sometimes our Christian walk seems a lot like a football game. Don't we look at our life and scream, "Bad call," when things don't go the way we planned? In our sinfulness don't we cry, "Look, Lord, I had everything planned out. Why did You let [insert your own dilemma here] happen? Bad call, God! You messed up! Just for that, You can count me out. I don't need You! What do you think of that?"

Brother, please remember that "[The LORD] loves righteousness and justice" (Psalm 33:5). It's so easy to miss how God loved us so much that instead of throwing a yellow flag on our life each time we sin, He penalized His own Son. Instead of denying us eternal life because of our many sins, He gave us eternal life through His Son's death (Romans 6:23). Sure, there's going to be bad calls in our life. But God never makes any bad calls. He does everything for our good. Once, He held out His right hand of justice against His Son. But now, because of Jesus, He extends that same hand out to us in forgiving grace.

God loved us so much that instead of throwing a yellow flag on our life each time we sin, He penalized His own Son.

Prayer: Dear God, forgive me for throwing penalty flags on Your play in my life. I deserve nothing but Your wrath. Thank You for sending Jesus, because through Him I know that "Your right hand shall hold me." In His name I pray. Amen.

Thursday

DAILY STUDY QUESTIONS
Psalm 139:9–10

1. In what way might a stadium on game day be thought to correspond to a far corner of the ocean?

2. Suppose you did dwell in a remote corner of the sea—marooned on a fertile but uninhabited island. What would be the hardest part?

3. In what ways would God's promise to sustain you with His right hand of blessing address even this need?

4. What does it mean to have God's right hand firmly hanging on to you and leading you? How do you know that God's hand is there?

5. Besides the delivery of justice and the giving of grace in Christ, name as many other benefits of God's guiding presence as you can in one minute.

Psalm 139:11–12

If I say, "Surely the darkness shall cover me, and the light about me be night," even the darkness is not dark to You; the night is bright as the day, for darkness is as light with You.

Into the Light

For me, night crawlers are synonymous with fishing. They remain the essential resource for my most productive fishing trips. Bluegill, sunfish, bullheads, and bass all find a hook baited with a night crawler too tempting to ignore. At times, I have experimented with earthworms and whole kernel corn, but the results were less than satisfactory. For one thing, I find it difficult to bait my hook with a run-of-the-mill earthworm. No matter how carefully I slide an earthworm onto my hook, I always manage to stick my finger. Moreover, corn flies off my hook whether the hook is barbed or not. One cast of the line sends kernels sailing, often hitting the water in three or four locations before my hook. As a result, the fish enjoy a corn appetizer while I'm left with an empty hook. My grandfather fished with a cane pole for years, but I never mastered his delicate touch. A simple wrist flick and he laid the bait in front of an unsuspecting fish; for me, the bigger the splash the better.

Most anglers buy night crawlers in a bait shop. Styrofoam bowls with plastic lids commonly hold a dozen of them. Commercial producers raise night crawlers to sell to bait shops. Bait shop owners buy them and resell them to anglers like me, often storing these bowls in an old refrigerator. Dark, cool conditions slow night crawlers down. Less active night crawlers stay within their Styrofoam environment. Although I usually buy night crawlers in bait shops, that was not always the case. At one point, I started hunting night crawlers. If you've ever done that, you know that "hunting" is the operative word. Hunting begins late at night and usually after a rain.

In today's reading, the psalmist notes, "If I say, 'Surely the darkness shall cover me, and the light about me be night'" (Psalm 139:11). When I read this verse, my thoughts immediately ran to nights spent in search of night crawlers.

When it came to knowing when to hunt night crawlers, my father had impeccable timing. Summer rains usually brought night crawlers out of their holes. My father said they came out to dry off and look for mates. If we were fortunate enough, sometimes night crawlers on their "honeymoon" meant that we got two worms for one. The tools needed for a successful hunt included a flashlight, a small bucket filled with earth (usually taken from a tilled spot before it rained), a strong back, quick hands, and patience.

In football, the field of play is an area 110 yards by 50 yards. In baseball, it's the diamond and outfield. In night crawler hunting, the mowed grass on either side of an alley offers the ideal playing surface. In football, eleven men form a team. In baseball, nine. In night crawler hunting, it's only two. One man holds the flashlight and bucket, while the second squats, stoops, and quickly grabs the night crawlers. The two men work in tandem. The team member with the flashlight works the light from fence line to alley in an easy motion. He never stops to shine a light directly on any exposed night crawler, since doing so results in the night crawler's quick exit into a nearby hole. After discovering a night crawler, the team member with the flashlight continues to move the light gently away until only a sliver of light illumines it. Gently, the second team member squats to grasp the night crawler between thumb and index finger. Sometimes the night crawler has slithered away from its hole a sufficient distance to make capture easy. Routinely, though, the second team member finds half the night crawler in its hole and half outside. In this case, a struggle ensues with the team member patiently, but firmly, wrestling to prevent one of two things from happening, either pulling the night crawler in half or losing it altogether. Neither is desirable.

For dad and me, a good night's hunt usually meant capturing two dozen. The number varied, depending on when we planned to fish and for how long. At the time, my grandfather had a lake at the south edge town. That meant we never had far to travel before reaching our favorite fishing hole. We stayed for hours, beginning late in the afternoon and continuing until the mosquitoes chased us home. One hearty night crawler easily baited three or four hooks when apportioned correctly. A nearby stock tank filled with fresh water supplied the perfect place for any fish we decided to take home later. Anyone fishing simply removed his or her fish from the hook while saving as much bait as possible. Grabbing the fish with thumb in the mouth and index finger under the "chin," the fortunate fisher retreated to the stock tank to deposit the fish.

Can we equate ourselves with night crawlers? Yes. Sinners (and that's you and me) believe that "surely the darkness shall cover me" (v. 11). Alone, we hide in our own darkness to conceal our evil deeds from God and others. If others cannot see it, our sins remain hidden, unexposed. Yet we don't stop there. Sometimes we hide additional misdeeds under cover of darkness. Despite our intentions to slither into the darkness, the light of God's Law exposes us for what we are: sinners. However, whereas anglers use a light to find night crawlers for bait, God shines His Gospel light on us in order to save.

Dear friend, if you are in a dark hole, isn't it time to leave it and come into the light? God's light not only exposes our sin, it also floods its beams on our Savior. Jesus made Himself a lowly worm by becoming a human like us, though without sin. He took our sins to the cross, where they pierced His hands and feet (Psalm 22:16). Jesus was "wounded for our transgressions; He was crushed for our iniquities; upon Him was the chastisement that brought us peace, and with His stripes we are healed" (Isaiah 53:5). Come into the light of Jesus' resurrection power and grace. Read again the inspired words of the psalmist, "Even the darkness is not dark to You; the night is bright as the day, for darkness is as light with You" (Psalm 139:12).

....

Jesus made Himself a lowly worm by becoming a human like us. He took our sin to the cross, where they pierced His hands and feet (Psalm 22:16).

Prayer: Heavenly Father, I often hide from You in the deep hole of my sin. Search me out with the light of Your Word. Wash me clean, and put me back on the right path of serving You and others. In Jesus' name. Amen.

....

Friday

DAILY STUDY QUESTIONS
Psalm 139:11-12

1. Is being in the dark a good thing or a bad thing?

2. How is hiding in the dark an accurate description not only of night crawlers but also of sinful man?

3. What does it mean that for God darkness and light are alike?

4. Is God's ability to penetrate the darkness with His gaze a source of comfort or of terror?

5. How is the image of being tugged out of safe hiding place (a hole!) in the ground an apt picture for the reality of what occurs in Baptism?

Week Six

....

PSALM 139

....

The 139th psalm is a psalm of thanks that
praises God that He has provided for them so
wonderfully and still reigns in all of His works,
words, and thoughts. Whether the psalmist
stands, walks, sleeps, or wakes— yes, even in
his mother's womb, before he was made— God
has been with him as he was being formed and
will be with him as long as he lives. It is as if
the psalmist should say: Every human ability or
power—how we live, what we do, speak, think,
wherever and whenever, from where we come
and to where we should go—it is all clearly
God's work and art.

– Martin Luther

Week Six, Psalm 139:1–12

GROUP BIBLE STUDY
(Questions and answers are on pp. 192–94.)

1. What is the farthest from home that you have ever been geographically? What about spiritually?

2. The women in our lives (mother, wife, and daughters) often possess the capacity to know us to the point of predicting our thoughts and actions with uncanny and alarming accuracy. How does it feel to be so thoroughly known?

3. If God knows the words you will say tomorrow at 9:37 a.m.—even before you know what they will be—then He clearly knows you better than you know yourself. What does this say about His ability to provide you with exactly what you need to follow Him and to thrive? How might this change the way that you respond to your circumstances?

4. What attributes of God does David illustrate with particular clarity and force?

5. One of the ways to understand Scripture is by using the distinction of Law and Gospel. What is the basic message of these twelve verses? Is it Law, or is it Gospel?

6. Most of the Old Testament writers don't disclose the fuller understanding of life after death revealed in the New Testament. In the Old Testament, they understood that the soul survived even death, but all souls together went to the netherworld known as Sheol. So, what is David confessing in the second half of verse 8? Is this a confession that a Christian would make (see Philippians 1:21–24; Romans 14:7–9)?

7. Is the picture of God revealed in Psalm 139 the image that most people today have of God? What sort of things fuel people's thinking about God today?

8. David's words are a fine example of Hebrew poetry, and in this instance some sense of the beauty of the text actually extends into the English translations. What portions of the text communicate to you in a significant way? What is it about the words that you find meaningful? Why might it be true that poetry actually communicates the wonder of God better than strict prose?

9. John picks up on the light and dark theme in the prologue of his Gospel (John 1:1–5). How does the revelation in John mesh with what David declares about light and dark (Psalm 139:11–12)?

10. What have you learned in the discussion and learning centered on this psalm that will make a difference in how you live the next twenty-four hours?

159

Small-Group Leader Guide

This guide will help guide you in discovering the truths of God's Word. It is not, however, exhaustive, nor is it designed to be read aloud during your session.

1. Before you begin, spend some time in prayer, asking God to strengthen your faith through a study of His Word. The Scriptures were written so that we might believe in Jesus Christ and have life in His name (John 20:31). Also, pray for participants by name.

2. Before your meeting, review the session material, read the Bible passages, and answer the questions in the spaces provided. Your familiarity with the session will give you confidence as you lead the group.

3. As a courtesy to participants, begin and end each session on time.

4. Have a Bible dictionary or similar resource handy to look up difficult or unfamiliar names, words, and places. Ask participants to help you in this task. Be sure that each participant has a Bible and a study guide.

5. Ask for volunteers to read introductory paragraphs and Bible passages. A simple "thank you" will encourage them to volunteer again.

6. See your role as a conversation facilitator rather than a lecturer. Don't be afraid to give participants time to answer questions. By name, thank each participant who answers; then invite other input. For example, you may say, "Thank you, Al. Would anyone else like to share?"

7. Now and then, summarize aloud what the group has learned by studying God's Word.

8. Remember that the questions provided are discussion starters. Allow participants to ask questions that relate to the session. However, keep discussions on track with the session.

9. Everyone is a learner! If you don't know the answer to a question, simply tell participants that you need time to look at more Scripture passages or to ask your pastor.

DAILY STUDY QUESTIONS

Monday   Psalm 112:1-2

1. The answer, as so often with such questions, is "Yes!" The praise of the Lord is the right context for reading and learning from the psalm.

2. Since the commandments are from God, and since they are a concise articulation of His will for the right functioning of His creation, they are inherently good. Those who live in God's way will learn to delight in the will of God, that is His commandments.

3. A blessed and mighty progeny is a worthy vision for a Christian man—and it is God's promise. This is the outcome for those who strive to live as God directs, that is, in the fear of the Lord.

4. Upright means doing things God's way. This happens only by grace through faith in Christ. One does not climb to this height but is raised there through faith and then strives to conform his living to the reality brought about by God's declaration of faith.

Tuesday   Psalm 112:3-4

1. Regardless of one's situation in life, wealth and riches are present—though perhaps not to the extent that we might prefer.

2. It does not feel good to feel "poor" when God has promised wealth. The key is to remember the promise of verse 4: in darkness, God brings light.

3. Clearly, the breaking in of light happens on God's timetable.

4. When our righteousness comes to us through faith in Christ, and is in fact actually the righteousness of Christ, then it does indeed endure forever.

Wednesday   Psalm 112:5-6

1. We know the feeling of being cheated but perhaps tend to forget the fact that our injustice inflicts these feelings on others.

2. Perfect justice is always giving to another what is his or her righteous due as a child of God. Certainly this means treating wife, children, parents, and fellow employees and drivers with justice—a bit more difficult than we may readily recognize.

3. Clearly none of us has truly lived the full extent of the Golden Rule—the pinnacle of just living—in every relationship.

4. The reach of sin is long and demanding. It is wise to deal truthfully with past failures.

5. Indeed, why not!?

Thursday   Psalm 112:7-8

1. A man's response to bad news varies with a multitude of factors. Oddly many people receive bad news with little reaction—internal or external. This may or may not be evidence of unwavering faith.

2. Strong and obvious reactions to bad news probably have more to do with personality than with a measure of faith. Even a healthy and vibrant Christian may break down in grief and suffering when receiving crushing news. This is simply the mark of being human. Even our Lord outwardly grieved at the death of Lazarus.

3. An emotionless response may actually send a message of apathy and indifference. Christians are not called to be stone-faced stoics in the face of disaster and difficulty. Confronted with severe challenges and devastating losses, the best Christian response may well be lamentation and mourning at the price of sin.

4. Perhaps the psalmist is not speaking about the actual reception of bad news as much as the debilitating fearful approach to life that results when one lives in perpetual worry about the possibility of receiving bad news. The righteous and blessed man will grieve when appropriate, but he will not spend his days living in dread and apprehension of receiving the bad news that will, admittedly, inevitably come.

5. In the twenty-first century, adversaries come in a wide variety of colors, sizes, shapes, and forms—some animate, some quite abstract. The comfort of the psalm is the reminder that in God's plan those adversaries that inject our lives with difficulty and sorrow will not have the last word.

Friday   Psalm 112:9-10

1. When we are honest, there is usually plenty in our lives to make us doubt a claim to personal righteousness.

2. Giving to the poor today (we would call it charity) is a good barometer of one's level of righteousness or ability to live according to God's will. Compassion is God's will, and one who is righteous will certainly show compassion. This is righ-

teousness considered from the standpoint of our human responsibility as creatures within God's creation, but it is not the end-all and be-all.

3. The key, of course, is to remember that righteousness is of two kinds: our own (which is always deficient) and that which we receive from God through Christ (which is always sufficient). The wonder is that in the fulfillment of God's plan at the Last Day, you will be fully righteous in both ways, and that reality will last forever.

4. Unpleasant and terrifying as the description is, it is the consistent scriptural image illustrating the destiny of the wicked. This should provide significant impetus to lead people to faith so that they might escape the damnation of the wicked—those who refuse to yield to God's will.

5. It could be for the comfort of those who are consistently being downtrodden by the wicked. It could also serve as a vivid contrast between the two classes of people in the world. One is either righteous (by faith, of course) or is counted among the wicked. There is no middle ground shoehorned between verses 9 and 10.

GROUP BIBLE STUDY
(Questions are on pp. 38–39.)

1. *What do you think of when you hear the word* righteous? *What does it mean to be righteous?*

Encourage the group to think beyond the expected standard Bible class answers. In regular life, what does it mean to be righteous? It is important to remember that in the Bible, righteousness is of two kinds. There is vertical or passive righteousness—the righteousness we receive from God by grace through faith in Jesus. And there is horizontal or active righteousness—the things that creatures do in service to one another that actually correspond with God's will.

2. *Describe the most righteous man you have ever known. What was his most compelling quality or characteristic?*

This is intended to be a nonthreatening question that should lubricate the group's willingness to talk and discuss. Give each participant an opportunity to respond with his thoughts.

3. *Is there a difference between being blessed and being righteous? Using the descriptions in the psalm, describe the characteristics of a man who is blessed and righteous.*

Essentially, no. Both describe the man who is rightly related to God through faith and rightly related to his fellow creatures by living according to the Creator's will. Tracing through the psalm, one gains a good idea of what God means by blessed and righteous.

4. *Verse 1 declares that the first two criteria of blessedness are fear of the Lord and delight in His commandments. What does it mean to "fear the Lord"? How do these ideas fit with a Christian perspective?*

Although it contradicts widely held ideas, in the biblical world, fear of God definitely included an element of good old-fashioned terror. Certainly we have reverence and awe of God, but it is good to recall that the universal experience of biblical characters is that an intense awareness of the presence of God provokes sheer terror (check out Isaiah 6:1–5; Luke 8:22–25; Revelation 1:12–18; and Matthew 10:28). As sinful human beings, we are rightly afraid of a just God. This fear unquestionably remains as long as we live in this broken flesh. As C. S. Lewis wonderfully reminds us: Aslan (our Lord!) is not safe.

5. *The psalm counts children as one of the marks of God's blessing. What is the correlation between a man's righteousness (the righteousness he achieves by his faithful living) and the success of his heirs? What is the definition or mark of a successful child?*

How a man raises his children has everything to do with the success they experience in life—especially when success is defined in a biblical and Christian way: one who walks in the will of God and ably serves those around him. God's definition of success is often at odds with the world's concept of the same.

6. *Consider verse 4. In what tangible ways does God bring His light into the darkness?*

Perhaps the best way to think about God's light is not so much insight into what to do in a dark or confusing situation as it is the light of God's promises actively present and working in the midst of dark and challenging times. The light of God that shines in our darkness is delivered with regularity and certitude in the Means of Grace: God's Word and Sacraments that bring us the promises of His gifts.

7. *The old saying "neither a borrower nor a lender be" seems to contradict the exhortation of verse 5. What is the value in being willing to lend? Why are we often reluctant to follow the psalmist's urging?*

A benevolent and generous spirit is the mark of a man who is living with the right priorities and values—he understands the place of things and the significance of people. The psalm also hints that lending brings its own reward even in this life, as others may be willing to vouch for the one who previously has blessed them with magnitude and grace. Clearly, our culture functions with a markedly different understanding about possessions and the dangers in lending.

8. *Jesus concurred with the words of verse 7 when He commanded us not to worry (Matthew 6:25–34)—not when receiving bad news and not when dreading bad news. What things might tempt a man to worry? How does a heart steadfast in the Lord aid in overcoming worry and fear?*

Responsibilities for family members and business dealings that impact that care probably make up the bulk of worry promoters, but there is undoubtedly a long list of potential sources of worry. Remembering that God is profoundly and perfectly in control is no small comfort during challenging seasons of life.

9. *Are verses 8 and 13 being somehow vindictive with their emphasis on looking with satisfaction on one's adversaries or enemies? How should a Christian understand this idea?*

When God triumphs, evil is vanquished. When our enemies are resisting God's ways, then their defeat is a cause of satisfaction that the truth has prevailed. It is not about revenge or payback but is a matter of standing for truth and celebrating its triumph. At the Red Sea, Israel rejoiced, but Egypt grieved. This reality holds also for the Christian, as the Book of Revelation makes abundantly clear (see for example Revelation 6:9–11).

10. *Think about the psalm's description of a righteous man, and name one thing that you will do this week to help you live righteously in one of those areas.*

Don't be generic! Think about lending, aiding the poor, raising children, living without worry and so on, and then offer a concrete action you will do in one of those areas that will be a demonstration of righteousness.

DAILY STUDY QUESTIONS

Monday Psalm 119:1

1. We don't use a word that never applies! Without fault or perfect are a couple of ways to think about being blameless.

2. Experts can limit their contact with the Law to intellectual study. Those who walk in the Law are immersed in striving to know and live it.

3. Scripture certainly assumes that a man can improve his ability to walk in God's Law by practicing. One does not simply decide that he's going to "do it God's way" and then be done with it. That decision to walk faithfully is followed by countless further decisions and daily effort.

4. The psalm gives no indication that he is speaking hypothetically. Blameless may be an ideal, but it is one for which we should all strive.

5. Each will know how best to honestly answer.

Tuesday Psalm 119:2–3

1. Testimony might lead one to think of a legal proceeding or to a testimonial about some person or product. It is helpful to remember that God's will for us is not arbitrary but ties directly to His own will—it is His testimony about us, His beloved creation.

2. The psalm assumes that to live for God is to live that way in a heartfelt, fully committed way. There is no halfway.

3. The problem with sincerity is that it is unattainable for fallen man. We live always with mixed motives and divided hearts—even when we strive to live simply and faithfully. Sincerity is not a human characteristic.

4. Yes. God desires our hearts, informing a high and right motive for godly living. In Christ, we get grace for our failed sincerity as well as grace to strive for something better.

5. Since Christ's righteousness has already been freely given to us, Christians should pursue the righteousness of this world—not for the sake of salvation but for the sake of the world and their witness to God's truth.

Wednesday Psalm 119:4–5

1. No doubt, every man can think of at least one time per week when he would appreciate a second chance at something he said or did.

2. Rules that change without notice whether on the road, in the office, or in our relationships can cause a tremendous amount of frustration.

3. That God's rules don't bend convicts us for our inability to honor them and also comforts us with the certainty of a sure guide that will not shift—at least we know what we are doing wrong. There are no surprises with God's Law.

4. God's mercy in Christ does not make sense according to the standard of the Law. Instead of justice (which can only mean condemnation) we are given mercy, forgiveness, and even new life.

5. Being given the chance for a second attempt is no guarantee of success; in fact, we can be sure that we won't be able to get even a do-over right on every try. God's grace in Christ's forgiveness is not dependent on us and our "improved performance."

Thursday Psalm 119:6–7

1. It is worth considering whether or not the shame we all feel from time to time is legitimate and correct or misguided and therefore in error.

2. While we are quick to tell others they have nothing to be ashamed about, the truth is that sin is a legitimate and healthy cause for shame. It was right for Adam and Eve to hide for shame after their sin in the Garden (Genesis 3:7–10).

3. It would mean that the one doing the looking is living in conformity with them. While it is obviously true that no man can do this fully and perfectly, that is not the point of the author of Psalm 119. He is suggesting that a man should be living according to the commandments of God and finding joy in the conformity and holiness that he sees.

4. The second use or function of the Law is not in question. The Law does always accuse because no man can live up to the unreachable heights of God's standards. But the Law also functions as the Christian's guide for living. Thus we do strive to live without shame—living in agreement with God's commandments.

5. Trained to distrust and even hate the Law, it is hard to imagine thanking God for making us aware of His commandments, but this is exactly the attitude of the psalmist . . . and the attitude of the Christian who is learning the joy of conforming all of his life to God's will.

Friday   Psalm 119:8

1. If God withdrew His sustaining hand from the world—even for an instant—then everything would collapse into chaos and nothingness. If He withdrew His hand from you, you would cease to exist.

2. Whatever the psalmist may be implying, we know that our appeal to God's sustaining mercy is never on the basis of what we have done but only because God has promised to be gracious to us.

3. Obviously, this assurance can have nothing to do with one's performance. Such certainty is grounded not in human actions or even human belief. Such certainty arises from faith in the unfailing promises of God.

4. Since Christ has been forsaken by His Father as the atoning sacrifice for our sin, we have nothing to fear. He was forsaken so that we will not be forsaken.

5. Rather than tracing a motivational link, why not simply acknowledge that the great gift of Christ's sacrificial work is that it frees us from the guilt and condemnation of our failure to live up to God's perfect standard? Freed from having to perform to achieve or win grace, we are at liberty to pursue a righteous life purely for the sake of those around us.

GROUP BIBLE STUDY
(Questions are on pp. 62–63.)

1. Psalm 119 is an acrostic poem. Each eight-verse section of the lengthy psalm begins with the same letter of the Hebrew alphabet. English also uses acrostics. How many does your group know?

The group knows more than it may realize. Try priming the pump with **G**od's **R**iches **A**t **C**hrist's **E**xpense, or **C**ompletely **U**seless **B**y **S**eptember (yes, this originates in St. Louis).

2. Hebrew poetry (the style of literature of the Psalms) is fond of parallelism (a statement or idea is reinforced by a second phrase that uses new imagery or vocabulary to say the same thing). What is the relationship between the two halves of verse 1?

The text seems to say that to be blameless is the same thing as walking in the way of the Lord, and this is no doubt true. One who walked consistently in the Law of the Lord would be blameless.

3. What overall impression does this section of the psalm present? Do you think that the psalmist actually expects his readers to keep the Law? How does this fit with your understanding of the Law?

The only honest answer is yes. This may be a bit disconcerting, especially if someone is operating under the assumption that the only legitimate purpose of the Law is to demonstrate our inability to keep it.

4. Often we are taught that the Law's real purpose is to show us our inability and our need for divine grace. How does the psalmist's persistent portrayal of the Law as a good and positive reality to be celebrated challenge this idea?

Clearly there is more to the Law of God than a hammer meant to crush. For the man who is righteous in Christ, the Law becomes the shape of his life, a source of joy, and a reason to praise God.

5. Consider verse 2. What do you think it means to seek God with all your heart? Why might it be argued that for fallen humans this is an impossible ideal?

Wholeheartedness means that one's whole life is devoted to the pursuit of God and His ways. In other words, one cannot give God a piece of one's life or focus on God for only a few hours out of a week. God consumes us entirely. As considered during the Tuesday questions, sincerity is a perilous commodity among broken human beings. We are at once sinner and saint, and a pure motive or an action unmixed with noble and ignoble purposes is quite impossible for us.

6. How does a man seek and secure a sincere heart that is purely focused only on God and His plans?

For this we can only seek God's mercy and rejoice to remember that what is impossible for us is fully within God's ability. While we are always mixed in our motives and actions, our Lord Jesus did what we could not do. Through Baptism we are joined to our Lord, and so He takes our failure and duplicity and gives us instead His victory, integrity, and righteousness. True righteousness comes only as a gift from God through Christ in the power of the Holy Spirit. In our lives, we can practice holiness and righteousness by our habits and our attitude toward daily living.

7. In verse five, the psalmist prays that his ways may be established. What does it mean to have one's ways established? What role does a man play in establishing his own ways?

Perhaps a good way to understand this is to consider Paul's exhortation in 1 Corinthians 4:16–17. Paul was confident that his ways were Christ's ways (1 Corinthians 11:1), and so he encouraged his readers to be like him and to live his way. This reminds us that establishing one's ways is at least in part an issue of habits and practices that one learns and does by intentional repetition. A life rightly lived does not happen by accident.

8. Think about verse 6. Why would a man be ashamed when looking at (that is hearing and studying) God's commandments? How can this shame be a good thing?

Shame is the correct result when one falls short of the standard—in this case the standard is God's perfect Law. Shame is an entirely fitting response to awareness of one's own failure to fulfill God's Law. This shame prompts repentance, which is the prerequisite to the delivery of God's grace. A man who is unashamed of his sin is not yet prepared to receive forgiveness.

9. What is something you have learned about God's Law for which you can give thanks today?

Hopefully, each participant will be able to recognize some aspect of God's truth (that is, His Law) that is particularly relevant to him.

10. What would you tell someone who is feeling forsaken by God?

The promise of Christ and His forgiving presence with us in Word and Sacrament is the only answer to feelings of God-forsakenness, which are quite common. Rather than trying to feel God's presence, we need to look to what our Lord has promised us. Clinging to His promise in spite of circumstances is a mark of Spirit-worked faith.

Week Three, Psalm 119:105-112

DAILY STUDY QUESTIONS

Monday Psalm 119:105

1. Most Christians are eager to see the hand of God in the circumstances of their lives and will conclude that God is at work by the "goodness" of the outcomes.

2. Sometimes what we thought was a good outcome evolves into a less than pleasant or even evil outcome. One must be careful not to equate good circumstances with God's pleasure or even God's will. It is always better and wiser to conform to God's will as revealed in Scripture.

3. Like all of God's people, he looks to the certainty of God's Word!

4. Since we can see nothing of the future, there is a sense in which it is accurate to say that our steps are always into the darkness of the unknown.

5. Verses 1 and 14 of John 1 assure us that Jesus is the Word. Simply knowing the forgiveness of Christ and the certainty of His promises is enough to bring light to the darkest paths we must tread. While the way forward may not be evident, Christ's presence brings light that comforts, reassures, and illumines.

Tuesday Psalm 119:106-107

1. Simply by living in this world as creatures, we have an obligation to live according to God's will for His creatures. As Christians who are rightly related to God, this is done with intentionality.

2. Each man should have a host of options from which to choose—don't miss the obvious areas such as family relationships.

3. It probably is not an increase in sin, per se, but an increase in one's awareness of sin. The more one knows of God's will, the more it is obvious that this will is not kept—not even close!

4. Keeping a sacred vow is no easy matter. Temptation afflicts the one who has promised, and if one should fail, the guilt is a source of exceeding affliction.

5. God has made His promise of grace readily available to all of His people. In Word (especially the spoken word of Absolution) and Sacrament, God delivers His reviving grace. Clearly, the best place to look for these gifts is where God has promised them to be—in His Church.

Wednesday   Psalm 119:108-109

1. It is good to reflect on the use of our speech and to realize just how much of it is wasted or even out of line with God's purposes.

2. When things are tough, we find ample excuses for compromising on God's Law.

3. This is likely a universal experience of men—especially in their closest relationships.

4. God's will as expressed in His Law is relevant to all of life, and keeping it in the forefront of your thoughts brings many rewards—like knowing how to stay out of trouble with your speech!

5. Make a plan to be deliberate about using your speech in productive and God-honoring ways today.

Thursday   Psalm 119:110-111

1. We are told specifically, of course. But in the Psalms, the wicked are those who refuse to acknowledge or follow God and His will for His creatures.

2. As the devotion notes, striving to follow God's ways may put one in situations that could be exploited by those who seek to embarrass and destroy God's people. However, God's man is also to use his wisdom to avoid such traps and to thwart evil schemes.

3. Living obediently according to God's Law is probably one of the best ways to avoid the traps and tricks of Satan.

4. God's Word—His guiding Law and His liberating Gospel—are the most precious things a man can possess (and he possesses them only by the grace of God). There can be no greater inheritance. And like an inheritance, this is a gift that can be passed on to one's descendants.

5. Obviously, it requires a unique man to be able to greet God's commands with joy. It takes a man who is graced by God's mercy and intent on living in God's reality.

Friday   Psalm 119:112

1. We still live in a broken world and still possess a rebellious old Adam who desires to live at odds with God's plans. Between the devil, the world, and our own flesh, we are bound to endure pain and suffering.

2. Two people, even two Christian people, may experience the same tragedy or setback with radically different outcomes in their character and life. The greatest factor is the mindset or worldview one has before, during, and after the incident, and this has much to do with a heart that is set on following God's ways.

3. It is useful to consider concrete situations and the alternative ways of meeting the challenges they present.

4. It isn't possible—at least not based on human shortcomings and our propensity to sin. Such promises can only be made in the context of God's grace and should be made with a fair amount of trepidation. Yet if ever there was an appropriate "forever promise," it would have to be the promise to follow God's ways always.

5. If you're drawing a blank, take a look at Exodus 20 or Matthew 5.

GROUP BIBLE STUDY
(Questions are on pp. 86–87.)

1. Has your community ever passed a new law that made an impact on your day-to-day life? What did you think of the law?

Maybe it was a new stop sign that interrupted your morning commute, a regulation that meant an expensive home improvement, or a law that required the purchase of bicycle helmets for your kids. You may have liked or loathed the law.

2. Every one of the 176 verses of Psalm 119 contains some term referring to God's revealed will. Pick out each word in the verses studied this week. What different connotations does each word carry?

The psalmist finds a wonderful array of words to refer to God's revealed will. Some that appear in this section are *word, rules, law, precepts, testimonies,* and *statutes.* While the words may have different connotations, in this psalm, they are essentially synonyms.

3. God's revealed will, the will of God for His creation, is more simply called the Law. How does a man learn this Law (see Romans 2:14–16; Deuteronomy 6:4–9)? Why do all men not universally recognize this Law?

Scripture teaches that the Law is both written on the heart of every man and also to be diligently and carefully taught. Sin clouds both methods of delivery, and so there is no complete understanding (let alone practice!) of this Law of God.

4. What is the psalmist's attitude toward the Law? What is different about the way that a Christian understands the Law (see Galatians 3:19–26; Romans 7:12)?

The Law functions in more than one way for the Christian. In Galatians, Paul stresses the way that the Law reveals our sin and convicts us of our failure and need for the Gospel. In Romans, Paul reminds us that the Law is not our problem or a bad thing. The Law is God's good, holy will, and our problem is sin that prevents our keeping of the Law. As God's holy will, the Law is useful to the Christian as a guide for living. Since the Law functions in such important ways for the Christian, we should be ready to join the psalmist in thanking God for the Law and in celebrating it with delight.

5. Calling God's Word a lamp and a light (v. 105) is an apt metaphor that has long been a favorite of believers. How many different ways can your group think of to apply the metaphor? In other words, in what ways is God's Word a lamp and a light?

Here are a few ideas to help the group get started: God's Word helps us make decisions about which way we should be when the way is dark and unclear. God's Word helps us see things and people around us more clearly—seeing them as God sees them. God's Word brings comfort and reassurance when we are frightened by the unknown.

6. *How does God's Word work to revive an afflicted soul? What role does weekly corporate worship (church!) and Bible study play in the revival of a soul?*

God's Word puts us back on track with who we are, who God is, and what He desires of us. All of these truths are inscribed on us during the weekly routine of worship and Bible study. Establishing this habit is establishing a life pattern of regular renewal and revival.

7. *What does James 3:7–12 teach us about the way we are to use our mouths? How might thinking about your words as a freewill offering to God (v. 108) help you to learn the lessons James wants us to learn?*

James challenges us to be consistent with our words and to recognize God's claim on all of our speaking. Considering each word as an offering acceptable and pleasing to God would likely do much to curb our harsh and discouraging speaking.

8. *How precarious is the life that you live? What sorts of snares are set in your path? Who puts them there? What kind of harm will they inflict? How dangerous are they?*

Most of us live relatively calm and secure lives, without any serious threats to our safety. Still, snares abound, placed there by Satan, by other people (sometimes well-meaning people, sometimes by friends and family), and by ourselves. These snares all threaten to stop us from following God's will. Every bit like a roadside bomb or IED, the snares in our path can wreak disaster in our lives, harm those around us, and even destroy life and faith itself. Sometimes the greatest danger doesn't look dangerous.

9. *In what sense is your Church (in all of its senses: congregation, denomination, and invisible Church—Militant and Triumphant) an inheritance that has been granted to you? What responsibility do you have to pass this inheritance to others? Are you leaving your children an inheritance equal to the one you received?*

God works through human institutions to communicate His truth and to spread His Gospel. Congregations and denominations are two of those institutions. We are responsible for how we care for these gifts of God, and we can impact negatively the inheritance that we leave those who follow. Perhaps we fail to remember that decisions we make with regard to the church and its practices and its message are decisions made for all subsequent generations who inherit what we have done.

10. *What things will you do this coming week to more fully incline your heart to know, do, and delight in God's Law?*

Whether it is reading daily from the Bible, Scripture memory, specific prayer for insight, or a more intentioned effort at instilling the inheritance in the next generation, each participant should be able to commit to one action that will positively influence his relationship with God's Law.

DAILY STUDY QUESTIONS

Monday Psalm 127:1

1. The interaction between human responsibility and divine provision is lively and complex. It is good to realize that both are always at work in every aspect of the Christian's life.

2. The common thread is that such labor is at cross-purposes with God's will.

3. Men are, by nature, good at "putting things together" and keeping a sharp eye on things. Both activities provide meaning and direction to the well-ordered (blessed!) life.

4. Recognize that threats to your Christian faith and life can come from an enormous variety of sources.

Tuesday Psalm 127:2

1. Some days bring more pain than others, but every day in a broken world has its challenges.

2. Give some thought to the physical and mental exertion demanded by an illness.

3. Ultimately, every human effort is eradicated by time and decay, and every human life ends in the futility of the grave.

4. While we give our full effort, we realize that success and meaning come only from God.

5. Whether the verse means that God gives sleep itself or gives gifts while we sleep is perhaps not important since both are true. In reality, sleep and rest are both goal and means.

Wednesday Psalm 127:3

1. This depends entirely on each man. Answers probably have varied over the course of each man's life.

2. Children are God's gift and should always be recognized as a blessing to be received with joy and determination.

3. A disposable culture extends its self-centered "keep life easy" attitude even to children, as is evident by the practice of abortion and the abuse of daycare as a surrogate parent.

4. One's investment increases dramatically with the recognition and appreciation of the value and significance of one's efforts.

5. Proverbs 22:6 indicates that the way a child is raised has everything to do with how a child turns out.

Thursday   Psalm 127:4

1. Arrows are necessary and useful. Thus, they are valuable. One can take the analogy further: each arrow is unique, each is the result of careful effort, the right use of the arrow takes practice, an arrow brings security, and so on.

2. Clearly, it does not. Small families are but one example of the different value placed on children, and one cannot simply dismiss the difference as attributable to an agrarian versus an urban/suburban culture.

3. A father's loving and careful direction are critical for the future success of a child. Minds and wills need training and directing.

4. A misfired arrow is the responsibility of the archer. Scripture clearly places responsibility for child-rearing failures on the father, even as it acknowledges an individual's (the child's) responsibility for his own choices and actions.

Friday   Psalm 127:5

1. This is something most twenty-first-century Christians are not asked to consider, but a strong case can be made that Christian families should be investing in the raising of children—as many as possible!

2. Highlighted are children, a place within the social order, and one's reputation.

3. As we know, we are identified by our family members, so a man's reputation has much to do with the way that man's children live.

4. Enemies may simply be those people who make life difficult, but regardless of the caliber of your enemies, God provides what you need to meet the challenge. He strengthens you with the Sacraments and equips you with His Word.

GROUP BIBLE STUDY
(Questions are on pp. 110-11.)

1. *What was the worst job you ever had? What was it about the job that made it the worst?*

This should spark a lively discussion. Not all labor is immediately satisfying.

2. *Psalm 127 breaks into two distinct parts. How would you describe the topic of each, and what is the relationship between them?*

The first portion focuses on work and the centrality of this aspect of a man's life. The second part is interested in a man's responsibility to raise children and the importance of that man trusting God in the effort. Together these two areas account for most of a godly man's attention. This is not to negate the responsibilities a man has to his wife, but they are not the focus of this psalm.

3. *Is Solomon being cynical (a charge often leveled at Ecclesiastes as well) in the first two verses of this psalm, suggesting that since there is no point to working hard (God is the one in charge anyway), why bother? If not cynicism, what is the motivation and message of these verses?*

The author of this psalm (and Ecclesiastes) is given to a healthy dose of realism bordering on pessimism. To an extent, this is a truth about life in this world—even for a Christian. However, a believer recognizes that God does bless life with meaning and does intervene to make human effort worthwhile and productive; there is no need for despair. Rather, the believer can be realistic about the oddities and inequities of hard work while still giving himself fully to his service within God's creation, knowing that his labor is not in vain, as Paul asserts in 1 Corinthians 15:58. Solomon seems to be urging his readers to keep a realistic perspective with regard to human toil and its importance.

4. *What is the right understanding of the relationship between human effort and divine activity? In other words, how can I be working hard at something when the success or failure of what I am doing depends entirely on God's intervention and activity?*

This is a recurrent issue in Christian doctrine. The answer is not entirely satisfying to human pride and curiosity. Basically, it boils down to this: humans are always held accountable for what they do or don't do in the accomplishment of their responsibilities, while at the same time only by God's will and mercy can any human project or effort ever succeed or produce fruit. It is one of the lively dynamics that undergirds the Christian life. The Christian man throws himself completely into his work, knowing full well that he is always dependent on God for any success.

5. *How are building and watching particularly apt descriptions of the work of a Christian man? What sorts of building projects occupy his attention? In what areas must a Christian man be an adept watchman?*

Don't limit these projects and activities to spiritual things, such as growing closer to God or watching for doctrinal error. It is important to remember that God is also God of the material world and that a man's work in that realm is important and godly. So, the building project may have to do with building a better marriage or family relationship, or it may deal with a literal building. All are of significance to God and deserve the careful attention of a godly man. The role of watchman is particularly critical in the home, where children need protection and direction.

6. *Why is it a matter of obedience and good stewardship to assure that times of hard labor are balanced with times of rest and sleep? Why have Christians sometimes had a hard time learning this? Do you think this is still an issue with people today?*

Jesus taught the need for rest (Mark 6:30–32). And God built a day of rest into the order of creation—six days of work followed by a day of rest. Clearly we are not to be machines that are to labor until they can do no more. Also, it is certain that rest makes labor easier and more productive. Perhaps there have been believers who have overemphasized the idea of the "work ethic" and have neglected the need for times of renewal and unadorned physical rest. Still, it is an open question whether in our leisure society Christians continue to suffer under this mistaken idea.

7. *Why would the psalmist so highly exalt the blessing of children? What are some of the blessings that come with having children?*

Our society denigrates the importance of caring for children and often portrays this work as a rather unpleasant burden. Help the group consider some of the many blessings that come with having children.

8. *Maternal instincts are well-known, and we have all seen the way that babies have a magnetic affect on women. What special roles do fathers have in the life of the children?*

Men need to be careful not to mostly relinquish the child-rearing task to women. The psalm provides excellent perspective on the importance of children and the critical task of the Christian man in raising children to be badges of honor to their father and their Lord.

9. *Christians are often eager to find Christ in every verse of the Bible—sometimes in spite of what the words might actually say. Think again about this psalm and consider where one may recognize the presence of Christ or truths that point to His truth.*

One must resist the temptation to allegorize, but it is probably fair to recognize Christological aspects of Psalm 127—even if they are not the dominant intended theme. The reminder of man's inability and his ultimate dependency push us to acknowledge our need for grace found fully in Christ. One may also make the connection between the child that honors his parent and the one Son who brings honor to His Father and so blesses all of us.

10. *What concrete, tangible changes does this psalm call you to make this week?*

Each member of the group should be encouraged to derive at least one substantive, concrete action that he will initiate in response to God's message in the psalm.

DAILY STUDY QUESTIONS

Monday   Psalm 128:1

1. It is good to recall that even in Scripture being blessed entails more than intangible spiritual benefits. It is the gift received when one is living rightly related to God and neighbor.

2. To fear God is to recognize and accede to the fact of one's insignificance and total dependence on God's mercy. Thus humility is a consistent mark of one who fears God.

3. When one conforms to God's will, that is, when he lives as God has directed in His Law, then he is living rightly related to both Creator and the rest of creation, and living this way, things simply tend to go better and to work. This is a simple and accurate understanding of what it means to be blessed.

4. One should seize with some relish the freedom to consider other images or metaphors for God and His relationship to His people. Many could be suggested, but the most effective are those that grow out of our own life experiences.

5. Each reader should be well aware of areas that particularly need his attention. God's Spirit both reveals those areas and guides us in their correction.

Tuesday   Psalm 128:2

1. All of our labor qualifies as sowing in view of a harvest. God is honored by a man's honest labor—it is what He created us to do, after all.

2. For most men, there are probably many harvest seasons or even harvest hours when it is clear that one's efforts have been worthwhile and effective.

3. The eschatological fulfillment of God's plan will bring the final and complete harvest. In a sense, all of the fruit that we enjoy now points to that day of final rejoicing.

4. Much of what brings us delight in our work and in our other efforts at godly living is not our own doing at all. God works through others and in ways we do not expect to accomplish wonderful fruit in our lives—a cause for gratitude and rejoicing.

5. It seems to be too typical that men hate their jobs. Yet in some sense, even

the most meaningless, insignificant, or distasteful job is still an opportunity to raise a harvest that honors God and gives cause for celebration.

Wednesday   Psalm 128:3

1. At times the images from the pages of the Bible don't exactly "click" in our culture, but the idea is clearly that a fruitful vine was a blessing!

2. Raising a successful crop, whether of grapes and olives or sons and daughters, takes a serious amount of planning, work, and commitment.

3. Like the man looking after his vine and his olive trees, a father must look after those under his care. Perhaps the psalm makes a point that needs more attention: a man is accountable for the well-being of all those under his roof and around his table. This is a task he must not abdicate.

4. At the table, we delight in God's bounty and celebrate the togetherness that we have. There each contributes and each receives. The kitchen table is a great blessing that deserves more intentional cultivation—as the psalmist recognized.

5. Think about your God-given responsibility not only to provide for but also to guide your family.

Thursday Psalm 128:4

1. Most of us probably have some memories of terrifying confrontations with a father's righteous justice levied against our sinful actions.

2. This is, indeed, the nature of our relationship with our heavenly Father and, as a reflection of that relationship, is the nature of our relationship with our earthly fathers as well.

3. Seeing ourselves rightly has everything to do with having a right understanding of where we fit. God is God, and we are creatures. God is in charge. He, and he alone, occupies the seat of authority. What life-changing pronouncements descend from his seat! He deserves our love, respect, and even fear.

4. We are rebellious creatures and challenge God's authority, question His plan, and resist His decisions for us. The ways this occurs defy numbering.

5. Only the man who is rightly related to God through faith in Christ can correctly understand all of the relationships that make up his life—most important, the relationship with his Creator and Lord.

Friday   Psalm 128:5-6

1. We know the impact of certain people (perhaps those in our own homes) on the equilibrium and plans of our lives.

2. It is good to be reminded again that we also leave a wake. None of us functions in a vacuum, and all of our actions and words have an impact on those around us.

3. Zion was the name of the hill on which the Jerusalem temple was built. Zion was the place of God's presence and blessing for His people. As a member of the new Israel (the people of God), the blessings of Zion and Jerusalem extend also to you.

4. It is a delight to see one's posterity taking shape, to see for yourself that the hard effort is producing excellent fruit. To see one's grandchildren is a gift of mercy.

5. The promise of peace appears often in the Bible. It is a mark of life being lived within God's plan. To know peace is the result of knowing God's activity and salvation in Christ. This peace is available in all circumstances and in every time and place.

GROUP BIBLE STUDY

(Questions are on pp. 134–35.)

1. *Tell about a time when you felt especially blessed. What was it that made that a blessed time?*

Perhaps it was a special time with family or a significant celebration or milestone, or maybe it was yesterday lived within the grace and plan of God.

2. *What is the difference between being blessed and being fortunate or lucky?*

Fortune and luck come by chance. Blessing is directed by One who is able to bless. In other words, blessing demands a God who is able to bless; luck can happen with or without a God.

3. *We are told (v. 1) to walk in God's ways. Are His ways the same for every one of us, or does He have a different way for each of us? What's the same, and what's different?*

God's ways are summarized in the Ten Commandments. This Law is God's will and so provides the "shoulders" or curbs marking the way of the Lord. This Law is the same for all of us. However, within the parameters of that way, there is much variety and options for us to choose our own unique way. Here, the criteria have to do with our obligation to fulfill our duties to those around us (vocation) coupled with our responsibility to use the gifts and abilities we have been given in service to God's creation (see the parable of the talents in Matthew 25:14–30).

4. *Is the work you do (at home or at your job) a curse or a blessing? How does God want us to understand our work (consider Genesis 2:15 and Ecclesiastes 9:10)?*

It is a blessing from God to be a productive member of His creation. Still, man's sin has caused even this blessing to be corrupted and made painful (Genesis 3:17–19).

5. *If we live in a broken world, and if sin pollutes and perverts everything, making our existence a vale of tears, how can a Christian man ever justify feeling happy?*

Life in this world takes place within a multitude of tensions—including the tension between the truth of sin and evil on one hand and the reality of God's activity and blessing on the other. So it is that we weep and grieve and rejoice and celebrate, and sometimes we do them all at once. The psalm reminds us that it is good and God pleasing to find satisfaction in a job well done and in a home thriving under God's favor (verses 2–3).

6. *How does a biblical view of the place and importance of the family differ from the view of the culture around us?*

Scripture understands the family as central and as the place within which God blesses and shapes His creatures. Established at creation (Genesis 2:24), the family is the essential building block for all of human society and functioning. Help the participants to consider the truth about society's attitude toward the family. The modern belief that family ties get in the way of individual happiness and productivity is evidenced by business expectations of travel and schedule that take no account of family, as well as by the popular "wisdom" that "for the sake of the kids" is not adequate reason to stay in a difficult marriage. A dismissive view of family and especially children is also evidenced in the assumption that children should not get in the way of my pursuit of individual happiness. This final point is even used as a rationale for abortion.

7. *What is a father's responsibility toward his wife and children? Why is it important to recognize a father's responsibility as much more than providing a roof overhead and food on the table?*

An aspect of our fear of the Lord definitely extends to family, and a father's responsibility is not fully accomplished when he brings home a paycheck and refrains from hanging out in bars. Children are to be brought up in the "discipline and instruction of the Lord" (Ephesians 6:4). This responsibility demands an enormous daily investment that is not met while spending time in front of the TV or on the golf course.

8. *Besides being indicative of long life, what is the blessing of living to see your "children's children"? How might this, in some circumstances, actually be a painful and unpleasant thing? What do your actions now have to do with which experience you have?*

To see one's progeny is to see the promises of God being realized. There is joy and contentment in the awareness that the work done in earlier years is continuing to bear fruit. Of course, all of this is negated when a child or grandchild willfully rejects his inheritance. A father's role in either preventing or fueling such a disaster is certain and not to be discounted or debated. (Though, it is also certain that no man may be held solely accountable for the choices and actions of another—even of his own child.)

9. *Zion, Jerusalem, and Israel do not have as much relevance for us as they did for those who used this psalm in the days of the Davidic kingdom and even down to the time of Jesus and Paul. What meaning might we take from these names today?*

Psalm 128 was part of the special group of psalms that made up the pilgrim songs used by those journeying to Jerusalem for annual festivals. To be blessed from Zion is to enjoy the blessing of God even during the homeward journey while praying that the next festival pilgrimage will grant another view of Jerusalem in its prosperity. As twenty-first-century Christians, we rejoice to realize that we are the new Israel (1 Peter 2:9–10; Romans 9:6–8) and are God's chosen people, the object of His great love and blessing.

10. *Decide on one thing you will do today at work or in your home that will enact in your life God's way of blessedness.*

This might be a different attitude about the value and meaning of work or an activity or special time spent with God's great gift of family. Whatever it is, come up with one thing you can do that will celebrate and promote a life that conforms to God's plan for the man who is blessed.

DAILY STUDY QUESTIONS

Monday   Psalm 139:1–4

1. This calls for some honesty. Keep in mind that God is not surprised by anything you might divulge to him. The exercise is for your benefit.

2. It is usually the cause of some anxiety and eventual fear (ultimately appropriate considering God's attitude toward sin) to become aware of God's complete knowing.

3. God is merciful, indeed, but He is also just—far more just than any human. It is sobering to consider the horror of God at the sin that we too often so casually commit.

4. God's knowledge of you means he knows it all: the pain, the fear, the sin, the need. It is at once convicting as well as comforting to be so thoroughly known. While no other human can truly understand your situation, God knows it better than you do.

5. See the answer to number 4.

Tuesday   Psalm 139:5–6

1. If you haven't yet had a close brush with disaster, consider how it would affect you to intimately experience the presence and plan of God and His intervening grace. An awareness of God's active care should do wonders for one's faith and attitude.

2. God's watchful presence in our lives is not always dramatic and palpable. And when we can offer reasonable human explanations for the things that occur, it is easy to think that God is not overly involved or doing anything special, when in fact, He continues to secure our faith and our lives.

3. David realizes that God is so completely in control and so thoroughly and surpassingly powerful that David is "blown away." But then the thought that is perhaps most remarkable (and the most humbling) is that this God is so intimately near that He completely surrounds David and even places His hand upon David. Indeed, who can comprehend being so perfectly known and loved by a God like our God?

4. It is good for our humility and our confidence in life to be compelled to think about how thoroughly "other" God is from us. He is not in any category that we can conceive; He simply eclipses any capacity of human thought. Meditating about such truths should prompt a man to pause and pray—for mercy and for sheer delight in the privilege of being known by such a God.

5. If God is reduced to being one's pal, much of God's nature is being missed. Such overfamiliarity with God can lead to a lack of depth in one's relationship with God, as well as a failure to appreciate the gravity of sin and the wrath of a holy God. The result is a god of our own making and a plastic relationship that is not grounded in reality.

Wednesday   Psalm 139:7-8

1. Faith leads us to recognize God's presence and activity even in the most trying and difficult situations.

2. David thinks of the farthest reaches of creation that he can imagine, and delights to confess that God is there. No one can ever outrun God—not geographically, not spiritually, not morally.

3. We expect to find God in heaven, but Sheol (the Old Testament underworld or place of the dead) is probably a bit of a surprise.

4. In death, we are still the Lord's and He is with us—rather, we are with Him!

5. Baptism is the gift of union with our Lord. We share in His death and His resurrection life. Those who are baptized into Christ are never away from their Lord.

Thursday   Psalm 139:9-10

1. A college football stadium on game day may not bear much resemblance to "the remotest part of the sea"—unless you are a member of the visiting team. Walking into that situation likely feels about as lonely and oppressive as dwelling on a forgotten island.

2. After establishing a means of survival, loneliness would probably be the driving concern.

3. Whatever the need, God's sustaining presence is sufficient to meet the need—but in sometimes surprising and unexpected ways.

4. The right hand is the hand of blessing. Often there is nothing tangible that one can name as evidence of God's hand of blessing. One does not always (ever?) feel the hand of God on his shoulder or even see signs of it in the unfolding of cir-

cumstances. The one sure reason for believing that God's hand remains is because He has promised it. God's promise is far more certain than any feeling or conviction we may have.

5. Everything in life is from the hand of God and can be rightly counted among the blessings of His right hand. It says much about human memory and focus that when pressed to name a blessing it so often happens that we can think of only a handful.

Friday   Psalm 139:11–12

1. Certainly, one's answer to this question depends on many factors. No doubt, it could be either depending on the immediate circumstances.

2. The dark provides the false comfort of anonymity and secrecy. In his sin, man craves both.

3. God has none of the limits that make dark and light polar opposites for humans. This means that God sees everything—even everything in the darkness—including the darkness of your secret sins.

4. God's attribute of omnipresence always cuts both ways. For the sinner, it is terror and conviction. For the soul caught in fear and despair, it is perfect comfort.

5. In Baptism, God lays claim on us and removes us from our comfortable place in a world of sin marked especially by self-absorbed living. In Baptism, we are given what we didn't even seek or desire. God delivers His grace to us actually in spite of us, because in our sinfulness, the sinners (yes, that's us) actually prefer sin and darkness to God's forgiveness and light.

Week Six, Psalm 139:1–12

GROUP BIBLE STUDY
(Questions are on pp. 158–59.)

1. *What is the farthest from home that you have ever been geographically? What about spiritually?*

The first question is safe and easily answered. The second requires reflection, though at this point in the study many participants will probably be ready to divulge their experiences of alienation from family.

2. *The women in our lives (mother, wife, and daughters) often possess the capacity to know us to the point of predicting our thoughts and actions with uncanny and alarming accuracy. How does it feel to be so thoroughly known?*

This common experience is probably at once comical, comforting, and convicting. It also serves to remind us that most of us men are not particularly complicated or complex. *Simple* and *male* seem to be virtually synonymous. At any rate, the knowing of our women pales next to God's knowledge of every part of us.

3. *If God knows the words you will say tomorrow at 9:37 a.m.—even before you know what they will be—then He clearly knows you better than you know yourself. What does this say about His ability to provide you with exactly what you need to follow Him and to thrive? How might this change the way that you respond to your circumstances?*

God brings into each of our lives exactly what we need to grow in faith and to use our gifts in fruitful service to others around us. He does not make mistakes and neither under- or overestimates our abilities and capacities.

4. *What attributes of God does David illustrate with particular clarity and force?*

Certainly God's omnipresence, omniscience, and omnipotence are presented with particular emphasis. These are characteristics that are God's very essence and that completely escape our capacity for comprehension—still, it is salutary to contemplate God's otherness and greatness.

5. *One of the ways to understand Scripture is by using the distinction of Law and Gospel. What is the basic message of these twelve verses? Is it Law, or is it Gospel?*

The basic message of this text is that God thoroughly knows every single solitary thing about you—every thought and every feeling, including all of those that you will have in the future. This message is at once Law and Gospel. It is Law to realize that every mixed motive and every dirty deed is fully exposed to God. It is Gospel to realize that nothing can ever take us from God's firm grasp and that no corner of creation is too far for God. He is always there.

6. *Most of the Old Testament writers don't disclose the fuller understanding of life after death revealed in the New Testament. In the Old Testament, they understand that the soul survived even death, but all souls together went to the netherworld known as Sheol. So, what is David confessing in the second half of verse 8? Is this a confession that a Christian would make (see Philippians 1:21–24; Romans 14:7–9)?*

David is saying, "Even if I die, You are there": a stark reminder of the futility of fleeing from God. Ironically, suicide is the worst way to attempt an escape from one's problems. Of all people, Christians can confess that in life or in death they abide with their Lord.

7. *Is the picture of God revealed in Psalm 139 the image that most people today have of God? What sort of things fuel people's thinking about God today?*

It might be observed that many people both in and out of the Church have a rather familiar view of God—sometimes to the point of looking at God as their buddy or "homeboy." David knew God's intimacy, but he also knew God's majesty and power—indeed God is to be properly feared as the one being in the universe deserving our abject terror! Where these ideas of a nonthreatening, easygoing, "I'm okay, and you're okay" God arise can be the topic of much discussion. But one thing to consider is the time-tested adage that the way one worships shapes the way one believes.

8. *David's words are a fine example of Hebrew poetry, and in this instance, some sense of the beauty of the text actually extends into the English translations. What portions of the text communicate to you in a significant way? What is it about the words that you find meaningful? Why might it be true that poetry actually communicates the wonder of God better than strict prose?*

Prose tends to become rigid and overly empirical, thus lending to the notion that our words can somehow capture the reality and harness the wonder of God, when such is absolutely not true. Poetry allows for a sense of the inadequacy of language to describe God's reality and forces us to recognize that the best we can do in talking about God is a series of images and experiences that evoke wonder, awe, fear, and praise—and all at once. While men tend not to be known for an affinity for poetry, with a little encouragement, most men should be able to find some portion of David's marvelous and lyrical words that resonate with their own thoughts and experiences.

9. *John picks up on the light and dark theme in the prologue of his Gospel (John 1:1–5). How does the revelation in John mesh with what David declares about light and dark (Psalm 139:11–12)?*

Already in the Old Testament, the Son (the preincarnate Christ) is actively at work—particularly in this psalm as He guards and protects David. God works according to His self-revelation in the Son, even in the Old Testament. Thus we recognize that light and dark are alike to God, because in Christ, God joins the darkness of this world and mightily overcomes that darkness. God does not soften the definitions or ease the requirements for the difference between darkness and light, He simply transforms the darkness with the glory of His presence. The darkness is no more.

10. *What have you learned in the discussion and learning centered on this psalm that will make a difference in how you live the next twenty-four hours?*

Each member should be able to articulate something that he can address in the next day or two. Help the group to remember that Bible study is not meant to be an end in itself. Knowledge of data is not the goal. Rather, a changed and continually growing life is the full outcome that each reader should recognize and seek. This is God's desire for each of His people.

A Guy's Guide to Church Lingo

Not everyone can tell a crankshaft from a camshaft, a rooster tail from a red worm, or a divot from a driver. You have to know the lingo (or at least know a mechanic, a bait-and-tackle guy, or a golf pro). Lingo is important, no matter the field, so here are some commonly used Church words and their definitions. Even if you are not already familiar with them, after studying them awhile, you should sound like a pro. Try this: "God has justified me through faith in His Son, Jesus Christ." That wasn't so hard, was it?

–The Editor

Absolve—*to set free from sin*. God absolves us in the Gospel and the Sacraments. Absolution is not merely a symbol. On Christ's behalf, the pastor absolves us after we confess our sins either publicly or privately.

Baptism—*a holy act using water and the Word*. Baptism is not merely a symbol. God truly forgives sins, gives His Holy Spirit, and creates new spiritual life in this Sacrament.

Bible—*God's Word*. There are sixty-six books in the Bible. Because the Holy Spirit inspired each of the Bible's authors to write down every word in the Bible, the Bible is without error.

Christ—*Anointed One* (Greek; in Hebrew: *Messiah*). *Christ* is a title, not Jesus' last name. Jesus is the fulfillment of God's promise to send His Spirit-anointed Son to save us from our sins.

Church—*community of the baptized*. Can also refer to a local congregation or the building in which Christian worship services are held.

Creation—*everything that God our Creator has made*. This includes all planets and stars and satellites, earth, animals, plants, human beings, and spiritual beings we cannot see, such as angels.

Cross—*instrument of torture and death*. By shedding His blood on the cross, Jesus paid the full penalty for our sins and guaranteed that we have God's free and full forgiveness.

Eternal life—*living forever in body and soul in a right relationship with God.* Baptized into Christ, we have God's promise of eternal life, even now in this life.

Faith—*God-given trust in His promises.* Through the Gospel and the Sacraments, God gives us the free gift of faith, which trusts in Jesus alone for salvation.

Forgiveness—*God's act of setting free from the guilt and penalty of sin.* Forgiveness is applied in the Gospel and the Sacraments. Forgiveness is received by all who believe that Jesus is their Savior.

God—*the unseen, almighty, eternal Creator of all that exists.* There is only one God: Father, Son, and Holy Spirit.

Good works—*good deeds.* Ultimately, God performs good works through believers, who are motivated and enabled by His love and forgiveness in Christ. True good works will be rewarded when Jesus returns.

Gospel—*the good news of forgiveness, life, peace, and joy in Jesus.* The Gospel centers on Jesus' incarnation, life, death, resurrection, ascension, and coming again.

Holy Spirit—*Third Person of the Trinity.* Through God's Word, the Holy Spirit guides, convicts, and comforts us with truth that our sins are forgiven for the sake of Jesus.

Jesus—*Son of God and Son of Mary.* Jesus lived, died, rose again from the dead, and ascended into heaven for us. One day He will return in glory for us. Jesus is 100 percent God and 100 percent man, although without sin. See *God.*

Justification—*declared in a right relationship with God.* We are justified through faith in Jesus Christ, our God and Savior.

Law—*what God commands or forbids.* The Law restricts outward behavior (curb), confronts us with our sins (mirror), and shows us how to live God's way (guide).

Lord's Supper—*holy act using bread, wine, and the Word.* Also called Holy Communion; the Eucharist. The Lord's Supper is not merely a symbol. Jesus gives us His true body and His true blood in, with, and under the forms of bread and wine to eat and to drink.

Pastor—literally *"shepherd."* God calls certain men to preach the Gospel and administer the Sacraments in His Church, most usually in a congregation.

Prayer—*communicating with God.* Prayer can be offered alone or with others, out loud privately, using written prayers, or simply from one's heart. God-pleasing prayers are sincere and are based on God's promises in His Word.

Psalms—*a collection of 150 hymns and poems in the Bible.* Written by David, Solomon, and other writers, many psalms were used in the public worship of Israel. Jesus frequently quoted from the Psalms.

Resurrection—*to rise bodily from the dead.* After dying on the cross, Jesus rose from the dead on Easter. When Jesus returns to earth, everyone who has ever lived will be raised from the dead. Those who have trusted in Him will be raised in perfect bodies that will never get sick, grow old, or die.

Sacrament—*holy act instituted by Jesus.* A sacrament is a sacred act instituted by God in which God Himself has joined His Word of promise to a visible element, and by which He offers, gives, and seals the forgiveness of sins earned by Christ. By this definition there are two sacraments: Holy Baptism and the Lord's Supper. Sometimes Holy Absolution is counted as a third sacrament, even though it has no divinely instituted visible element.

Salvation—*deliverance.* To be saved means to be delivered from sin, Satan, and death. Jesus is our Savior; He freely gives us His salvation through the Gospel and the Sacraments.

Sanctification—*to be made holy.* After God declares us holy (justification), He makes us holy (sanctification) through the Gospel and the Sacraments, so that we begin to do good works in His sight.

Sin—*disobedience of God's Law.* Since Adam and Eve, all humans are born under God's condemnation for the sin that dwells within them, which leads them to commit actual sins. The only way to remove the guilt and penalty of sin is through God's forgiveness.

Son of God—*Second Person of the Trinity.* Jesus is both the Son of God and true man, in one person.

Trinity—"tri-unity," *Three in One.* The Father, the Son, and the Holy Spirit are one God. See *God.*

Word—*God's revelation of Himself.* The Bible is God's Word; Jesus, as the Son of God, is God's Word in human flesh.

Worship—*receiving and responding to God's gifts.* God gives us His Word and Sacraments, and we respond to Him with prayers, praise, thanksgiving, offerings, and lives of service.